MW00412645

THE CHRISTLIKE LEADER

"*The Christlike Leader* is full of inspirational and practical advice for Church leaders. The writing makes even complex leadership concepts clear and accessible. Through examples from the scriptures, other Church leaders, and his own rich Church and professional leadership experience, the author illustrates leadership principles that are inspired and practical. I believe that both the novice and the experienced leader will find ways to become more effective as they consider how to apply these concepts and principles and lead the way the Savior led."

—**Alan L. Wilkins**, academic vice president of Brigham Young University, 1996–2004

"I wish I'd had this book when I was training leaders as a member of the Relief Society General Board. Kimball Fisher has done a masterful job organizing the essential principles of Christlike leadership and presenting them in a format that is extremely useful and easy to access. His thoughtful outline is an excellent guide for both the learner and the teacher. The scriptural and personal examples are inspirational and heartfelt. This book can be a blessing to seasoned leaders as well as those who are new to the demands of leading."

—**Connie D. Cannon**, Relief Society General Board, 2002–07

"The Church needs effective leaders today more than ever—leaders who are close to the Spirit, innovative, and filled with love. Kimball Fisher has created a groundbreaking book that will help leaders experience breakthroughs in their stewardships. He accomplishes this with an incredible focus on one simple idea: lead like Jesus Christ. This book is thought-provoking and filled with practical applications. Fisher's focus on becoming Christlike servant-leaders will foster change and effectiveness when applied at any level of Church leadership."

—**David M. R. Covey**, author of *The Highly Effective Missionary*

THE
CHRISTLIKE
LEADER

foreword by LEE TOM PERRY

THE
CHRISTLIKE
LEADER

KIMBALL
FISHER

CFI
An Imprint of Cedar Fort, Inc.
Springville, Utah

ISBN 13: 978-1-4621-1675-1

Published by CFI, an imprint of Cedar Fort, Inc.
2373 W. 700 S., Springville, UT 84663
Distributed by Cedar Fort, Inc., www.cedarfort.com

LIBRARY OF CONGRESS CATALOGING-IN-PUBLICATION DATA

Kimball, Fisher, author.
The Christlike leader / Kimball Fisher.
    pages cm
Includes bibliographical references.
ISBN 978-1-4621-1675-1 (perfect bound : alk. paper)
1. Leadership--Religious aspects--Church of Jesus Christ of Latter-day Saints. I. Title.

BX8643.L4K56 2015
253--dc23

2015030264

Cover design by Shawnda T. Craig
Cover design © 2015 Cedar Fort, Inc.
Edited and typeset by Kevin Haws

Printed in the United States of America

10 9 8 7 6 5 4 3 2 1

Printed on acid-free paper

For my sweetheart, Reenie

Contents

"And he saith unto them, Follow me, and I will make you fishers of men" (Matthew 4:19).

Contents

FOREWORDS

*I*t's like nailing jello to a wall." That's what some of my exasperated students said about leadership after studying many leadership theories and trying to identify their commonalities. I have a colleague who has read ten times as many books about leadership as I have, and he merely shakes his head at the mind-numbing clutter of ideas and continues to read, as if the next new book about leadership will finally solve the puzzle. Akio Morita, the former CEO of Sony, used to call organizations "fate-sharing vessels," and everyone who wants to understand leadership shares this similar fate—they are like Soren Kierkegaard's knight, who is chasing after a rare bird. Each time he reaches out to catch it, the bird escapes.

Kimball Fisher's book *The Christlike Leader* will not be the last book anyone who is fascinated by the subject of leadership will read. It, however, is a rare and valuable book for three reasons. First, the reason leadership is a difficult subject to nail down is it is nearly as much about style as substance. Kimball focuses on a specific style of leadership: the Savior's. Like one of the Savior's disciples, Kimball listens and observes the leader whose style he seeks to emulate. Mortal minds are not good at reading God's mind, but Kimball draws valuable insights because he strives to study, listen, and learn from Christ's example as a leader. The task is a bit like translating a difficult text, and while no translation is ever perfect, Kimball's is insightful, helpful, and ultimately satisfying.

Second, the book is based on many years of experience, during which Kimball has strived to lead as Christ led. I am of the school of thought that the best that any of us can do to emulate God is to strive to be like Him. Only He is the perfect leader. Many of us will experience a rare moment when the Spirit testifies to us that we have done as He would do, led as He would lead. We receive the divine accolade: "Well done, thou good and faithful servant" (Matthew 25:21). However, I do not know any priesthood or Church leader who has never been frustrated with his or her shortcomings, especially when aspirations are set by the Lord's standards—at a height none of us can consistently clear. This is the way we test the limits of all that we can do so the Savior can do the rest (see 2 Nephi 25:23). The school of striving is the best school to attend to understand Christlike leadership, and I believe Kimball is among the school's honors students.

Finally, Kimball has studied what others—some of them prophets, seers, and revelators—have written about Christlike leadership. He has performed a tremendous service by blending the insights of others about Christlike leadership with his own. I find that I can read on this subject over and over again and still not quite get it. I need books like this book to sustain my striving. It teaches me about the flaws and imperfections in the style and substance of my leadership in an encouraging and hopeful way. While I cannot seem to keep everything in the book in my head at once, it motivates me to improve one principle at a time. In the process, I am reassured that my leadership trends more upward than downward, and I have confidence that my knowledge of the Lord's way is increasing over time.

I read *The Christlike Leader* quickly the first time, but I intend to reread it slowly—perhaps a chapter a week—savoring all of it, and choosing a few of its insights to apply to improve my leadership. I am assuming that some of Kimball's insights will fit me better than others, but his book offers an assortment of shapes and sizes, and some of them are bound to fit me perfectly.

—**Lee Tom Perry**, dean of the Marriott School of Management at Brigham Young University; author of *Righteous Influence: What Every Leader Should Know about Drawing on the Powers of Heaven*

A<i>nyone who has</i> studied the life of Jesus Christ is struck with the wisdom and love with which He performed His ministry. He was constantly lifting and inspiring those around Him. Insights into His style of leadership, however, require much closer scrutiny to fully appreciate. When He said, "I am the way, the truth, and the life" (John 14:6), He was inviting us to take a closer look.

This book is filled with personal examples from Kimball Fisher's life and from the lives of others demonstrating practical leadership solutions. These solutions were gleaned by counseling with others, studying the lives of current and past spiritual leaders, and, of course, by considering the Savior's approach to solving similar problems. Charts and illustrations are included throughout the book, which highlight considerations with various situations, and are enlightening.

One helpful discussion focuses on the fact that good leaders must learn to minister and administer effectively. This is true when working with individuals and councils. Showing how the Savior performed both functions is rather revealing.

Kimball correctly points out that being converted to the Savior's type of life—the idea of *being* more than doing—is vital to understanding His type of leadership. I have known Kimball Fisher for many years as a Church leader and friend. His knowledge of sound management principles is evident in how he serves and teaches. The Christlike life he lives is one of the best endorsements for him discussing how to *be* a Christlike leader.

The chapter on helping people deal with trials and tragedy is especially insightful. All leaders face the challenge of comforting in times of need. Learning how to love as the Savior did and help others apply the enabling power of His Atonement is invaluable.

Kimball concludes this outstanding work with the statement, "The Savior is an exemplar, scholar, believer, seeker, disciple, teacher, and shepherd. By following Him, we can improve our leadership abilities to help those we serve return to our Father in Heaven." This inspiring book encourages better leadership by looking more closely at the Savior, Jesus Christ, the best of all.

—**Marvin T. Brinkerhoff**, Area Seventy, 2007–12;
president of the Idaho Pocatello Mission, 2012–15

ACKNOWLEDGMENTS

My *father and* mother, Chad Kimball Fisher and Patricia Anne Fisher, taught me much of what I know about leadership. Like Nephi, I was born of goodly parents too.

Numerous other people throughout my life have helped me learn what it means to lead, in particular my advisors as a student body officer in middle school and high school, my Scoutmaster Ross Olsen, seminary teachers, Young Men's leaders, and bishops (especially Kay Phippen). I'm also grateful for the crucial lessons I learned later in the Japan Sapporo Mission and in wards and stakes spread across Utah, Ohio, Illinois, Washington, and Oregon, where I've been blessed to serve with many remarkable men and women in most of the ward and stake leadership councils.

Academically, I studied leadership at Brigham Young University in what was then called the masters of organizational behavior program in the Marriott School of Management. I learned from renowned scholars, including Bonner Ritchie, Bill Dyer, Warner Woodworth, Alan Wilkins, Paul Thompson, Gene Dalton, Steve Covey, and Kate Kirkham. This distinctive program enlisted superb faculty with Christlike values and molded my thinking about leaders dramatically.

There I also met my eternal companion, Mareen Duncan Fisher, with whom I first studied leadership, and who would eventually become my business partner in a consulting and training firm to teach leadership principles and practices to others professionally. No one has had a more powerful effect on my understanding and application of leadership than my eternal partner, Reenie, with whom I have served for more than twenty years to train business, university, Church, and government managers how to be more effective leaders. I thank the Lord for her every single day.

My business colleagues at Procter and Gamble, and Tektronix, taught me much about applying effective leadership practices in the business world. I am indebted to them, and to those who would later become our clients, for lessons too numerous to recount.

I'm especially appreciative of the wonderful team at Cedar Fort publishing for their assistance on this book. Thanks to Bryce Mortimer and Emily Chambers for believing in this project; Shawnda Craig for the amazing cover; my wonderful editor McKell Parsons for her powerful insights, with copyeditor Kevin Haws, for their tireless massaging of the manuscript; and Kelly Martinez for his awesome marketing support. It really takes a village to make a book!

This work and its flaws are entirely my doing. The book does not represent the official view of The Church of Jesus Christ of Latter-day Saints, and I accept full responsibility for any doctrinal, historical, or professional errors or misinterpretations contained herein. As I launch it out into the world, I feel a little like the prophet Moroni in the Book of Mormon, who wrote, "Condemn me not because of mine imperfection . . . but rather give thanks unto God that he hath made manifest unto you our imperfections, that ye may learn to be more wise than we have been" (Mormon 9:31).

Despite its weaknesses, it is my fervent prayer that this work may help new Church leaders emulate the powerful practices of the most perfect leader in history. There simply isn't a better example to follow than our Savior, Jesus Christ.

INTRODUCTION

"Wherefore, follow me, and do the things
which ye have seen me do" (2 Nephi 31:12)

My first act as a Church leader was a colossal failure. I was twelve years old and had just become the leader of the Panther patrol in Boy Scout Troop 391 of the Valley View Eighth Ward in Holladay, Utah. Excited by my new assignment, I was anxious to do well, but I wasn't really sure how to lead.

I decided that the first thing I was going to do was get my friend Gary to come to the next patrol meeting. He hadn't been participating regularly, and I missed him. Imbued with a puffed-up sense of self-importance from my new calling, I felt sure that all I had to do was call Gary and tell him to come. After all, I was the patrol leader. The boss. I could *make him* want to become an active part of our patrol.

I called him. "Gary," I said, "I want you to come to our next patrol meeting." He said no. I was flabbergasted. How could he possibly decline? I was his leader. "Just be there," I ordered and hung up. I was too inexperienced to recognize that the Spirit left at the moment that I tried to coerce Gary, too new in my knowledge of the gospel to realize that this tactic was inconsistent with its teachings, and too naïve about leadership to understand the futility of force. I actually assumed he would show up at the meeting.

He didn't. But I remember spending much of my time watching the door, waiting for him to come through it.

At some level, I knew that what I had done as Gary's patrol leader was wrong. A lesson from a wonderful Primary teacher came to my mind. She had told us that whenever we had a difficult situation in our lives, we should ask ourselves the question, "What would Jesus do?" As I thought about what I had done, I realized that it had not been Christlike. That simple Primary question ended up being a great guide as I later served in a variety of leadership assignments in my home, mission, ward, and stake.

What would Jesus do?

President Thomas S. Monson shared an instructive personal experience that reinforces this idea in the October 2004 general conference. From the time of his calling as a twenty-two-year-old bishop, he has kept a Heinrich Hofmann print of the Savior on the wall of his office across from his desk. "Whenever I have a difficult decision to make," he said, "I have looked at that picture and asked myself, 'What would He do?' Then I try to do it. We can never go wrong when we choose to follow the Savior" ("Choose You This Day," *Ensign*, November 2004).

If we examine the life and teachings of the Savior, we find all of the essential leadership lessons to help us be more effective in our callings and our lives. In the following chapters, we'll review these leadership lessons in more detail, examining how He acted as a servant-leader; how He served as an exemplar and scriptorian; and how He prioritized, communicated, motivated, delegated, ministered, taught, and corrected others. Though these leadership lessons are all interwoven into the rich tapestry of the gospel, examining each thread independently will allow us to see how to apply His example to specific situations in our own callings.

In his important Church leadership book, *Righteous Influence: What Every Leader Should Know about Drawing on the Powers of Heaven*, Brother Lee Perry emphasized another reason for emulating the Savior. He noted that great leaders such as Paul and John the Baptist realized that it was not their own works but the Lord working through them that gave them the authority and power to lead effectively. Expounding on this, Brother Perry wrote, "It is Christ's power working through leaders that enables ordinary men, women, and youth to do extraordinary things" (*Righteous Influence: What Every Leader Should Know about Drawing on the Powers of Heaven* [Salt Lake City: Deseret Book, 2004]). Being a Christlike leader can enable us to not only develop the Christlike skills that make us better leaders but also the divine power to accomplish more than we are mortally capable of doing alone.

These leadership lessons are important for all of us, whether we currently serve as youth or auxiliary leaders, bishops, or Relief Society presidents. As active Latter-day Saints, we will all likely have an opportunity to serve in a ward or stake leadership council at some point in our lives.

When Kim Clark was the dean of the prestigious Harvard Business School, an institution famous for educating some of the most important leaders in the world, a colleague stopped him one day to ask a question. After noting the six LDS educators who taught at the business school and the many LDS students—a significant over-representation of such a relatively small population—he asked, "Why are so many Mormons good leaders?" Brother Clark answered, "We get lots of experience" ("Leadership," *Mormon Channel Radio*, Episode 29, October 2011).

As active Church members, we do get lots of experience leading others—more than most people do. We get crucial leadership experience, even if we are never called to serve in the executive councils of our auxiliaries, wards, or stakes. Why? Because our Church teaches that effective leadership in our families is *the* critical leadership assignment of mortality. As President Spencer W. Kimball taught, "[Parenthood] is leadership, the most important kind of leadership" ("The Example of Abraham," *Ensign*, June 1975).

Our most significant responsibility in life is to first lead ourselves, and then our families, back to Heavenly Father. All other callings wilt in comparison. If we are ever to serve as husbands or wives, mothers or fathers, grandparents, uncles, aunts, or older brothers or sisters, we need to learn how to become Christlike leaders.

CHAPTER ONE: HOW TO
BECOME CONVERTED

"And when thou art converted, strengthen
thy brethren" (Luke 22:32)

*A**s a young** man*, I learned a number of important leadership lessons from serving in my Scout troop and Aaronic Priesthood quorums. For example, my deacons quorum advisor taught me how to run meetings using an agenda. My Scoutmaster taught me how to create a project plan, make specific assignments, and follow up on them. My father showed me how to change my language to minimize judgmental *you* statements (for example, "You should turn in your fast offerings to the bishop as soon as possible," or, "You need to read the scriptures daily") and use more inclusive *we* statements (for example, "We need to turn in our fast offerings more quickly," or, "We need to read our scriptures daily"). My mother helped me understand that the people I led needed to know I cared about them, and that sometimes I had to sacrifice the accomplishment of a task to demonstrate compassion or build relationships.

As a result of these lessons, I began to feel more comfortable as a leader. I even sought out opportunities to become a student body officer in my middle school and high school. But I don't think I understood that learning the techniques of leadership doesn't make someone a leader. I thought that leadership was something you *did*, rather than something you *were*.

Christlike Leadership Requires Conversion

Perhaps this is the great lesson Christ was teaching Peter (often referred to as Simon in the Gospels) in the book of Luke: "And the Lord said, Simon, Simon, behold, Satan hath desired to have you, that he may sift you as wheat: But I have prayed for thee, that thy faith fail not: and when thou art converted, strengthen thy brethren" (Luke 22:31–32).

I imagine the words of the Savior may have stung Peter. Perhaps he thought, *But I am converted. How can thou doubt my faith? Look at what I have done. I followed thee, gave up my vocation, and made it my life's mission to be thy disciple. I have been witness to thy miracles. I have seen thee heal the sick and raise the dead. At thy bidding, I even briefly walked on water.*

The scripture continues with Peter's objection: "And he said unto him, Lord, I *am* ready to go with thee, both into prison, and to death" (Luke 22:33; emphasis added).

But the Lord knew that despite Peter's valiant efforts and good intentions, he had not yet become fully converted. He still cared more about the things of the world than the kingdom of God, as noted in Matthew 16:23, when the Savior "turned, and said unto Peter, Get thee behind me, Satan: thou art an offence unto me: for thou savourest not the things that be of God, but those that be of men." Sadly, the Lord then prophesied, "I tell thee, Peter, the cock shall not crow this day, before that thou shalt thrice deny that thou knowest me" (Luke 22:34).

As we know, the prophecy was fulfilled with exactness: "And Peter remembered the word of Jesus, which said unto him, Before the cock crow, thou shalt deny me thrice. And he went out, and wept bitterly" (Matthew 26:75).

Though Peter's betrayal of the Savior didn't rise to the level of Judas that is described just a few verses later, it must have humiliated him. How could he serve as an effective leader in the Church of Jesus Christ, whom he thrice was unable to publicly acknowledge even knowing?

Peter couldn't do everything required of him as a Church leader until he was truly converted. And so it is with us. Conversion is the only prerequisite for becoming a true Christlike leader; no other education or experience is necessary.

What Is Conversion?

Learning leadership skills or techniques without this prerequisite wouldn't have made much difference to Peter's leadership effectiveness. It won't make much difference for us either. Regardless of our callings, the requirements of Church leadership are difficult, if not impossible, for those of us who are not yet fully converted. How can we lead others to places we have never gone? How can we draw from the reservoir of testimony, compassion, and commitment accessible only to those who care more about building the kingdom of God than bowing to peer pressure or relying on the arm of flesh?

Remember the story of the people of King Benjamin? The king wanted his people to become converted: "For the natural man is an enemy to God, and has been from the fall of Adam, and will be, forever and ever, unless he yields to the enticings of the Holy Spirit, and putteth off the natural man and becometh a saint through the atonement of Christ the Lord, and becometh as a child, submissive, meek, humble, patient, full of love, willing to submit to all things which the Lord seeth fit to inflict upon him, even as a child doth submit to his father" (Mosiah 3:19).

I've summarized the differences between the characteristics of what the scriptures call the natural or unconverted man or woman and the saint or converted man or woman in Figure 1-1 below.

Figure 1-1: The Natural Man versus the Saint

Natural Man	Saint
Doesn't rely on Spirit	Yields to enticings of the Spirit
Unrepentant	Applies the Atonement
Jaded or childish	Childlike
Disobedient	Submissive
Overbearing	Meek
Proud	Humble
Impatient	Patient
Apathetic or hateful	Full of love
Unwilling to submit to God	Willing to submit to God
Wants to do evil	Wants to do good continually

Not everyone who receives a leadership calling will be converted at the time of his or her calling. I certainly wasn't as a thirteen-year-old deacons quorum president. Even Peter, who would later become the senior Apostle of the Church, apparently wasn't fully converted when he was originally called to serve the Lord.

However, while being unconverted doesn't disqualify us from serving (after all, the Lord didn't release Peter as an Apostle), the full power of Christlike leadership is unavailable to us as "natural" men and women. As we read in Paul's admonition to the Corinthians, "But the natural man receiveth not the things of the Spirit of God: for they are foolishness unto him: neither can he know them, because they are spiritually discerned" (1 Corinthians 2:14).

It is unlikely that we can have the power to strengthen others until we are ourselves strong in the faith as true Latter-day Saints, worthy to be directed by the Spirit.

How Does Conversion Happen?

So how do we become converted? We study diligently, keep the commandments, and obtain a testimony. We ask for the Spirit to confirm the truthfulness of the gospel to us. My favorite scripture on the subject is found in Alma 32, where the great prophet Alma the Younger shows how building faith is like planting seeds. It's a must-read if you are early in the conversion process.

Though conversion can happen quickly, for most it takes time. And even after we are converted, we will still make mistakes that require repentance. But once converted, we begin to desire the things of God more than the things of man. We think about eternity more than just our temporal existence. We desire good more than evil to be more like the Savior.

We experience a change of heart similar to that of the people of King Benjamin: "And they all cried with one voice, saying: Yea, we believe all the words which thou hast spoken unto us; and also, we know of their surety and truth, because of the Spirit of the Lord Omnipotent, which has wrought a mighty change in us, or in our hearts, that we have no more disposition to do evil, but to do good continually" (Mosiah 5:2).

Summary

True conversion is a prerequisite to becoming a Christlike leader; it's the foundation on which we build our personal leadership practice. However, before we review the specifics of what we can learn about leadership from the life of the Savior, let's consider in the next chapter how Church callings differ from secular leadership positions.

Chapter Two: How Church Leadership Differs from Secular Leadership

"But Jesus called them unto him, and said, Ye know that the princes of the Gentiles exercise dominion over them, and they that are great exercise authority upon them. But it shall not be so among you: but whosoever will be great among you, let him be your minister; and whosoever will be chief among you, let him be your servant" (Matthew 20:25–27)

Though a member all my life, I wasn't truly converted until I attended college. I felt a strong desire at that time to become a missionary and received a call to serve in the Japan Sapporo Mission. I enjoyed my mission and had several leadership callings. While serving as a zone leader, I began to hope that the Lord would call me to work as an assistant to the president. But I noticed that the warm and comforting feeling I had come to know was the Spirit would withdraw when I thought about my aspirations for a "higher" position. I came to realize that this type of ambition was a form of pride, the dangerous disease that so often beset the Nephites in the Book of Mormon prior to a devastating fall.

Church leadership callings differ from secular leadership positions in this way. As President Uchtdorf said, "We do not seek, nor do we decline, callings that come from God through inspired priesthood channels" ("Faith of Our Father," *Ensign*, May 2008).

This is contrary to what I would learn about secular leadership later in management school. In the business world, a lack of ambition can be viewed as a weakness. Employees are expected to rise to the peak of their capabilities. Ideally, those who are perceived as the most qualified are rewarded with promotions to greater and greater heights of responsibility and power, limited only by their skills or motivation. There is a certain order that is achieved from this hierarchy of people and tasks.

Leadership callings in our faith, however, are not based on the secular notions of meritocracy or hierarchy espoused in the business or government organizations where I have spent my career. The scriptures clarify that we are called "not according to our works, but according to his own purpose and grace" (2 Timothy 1:9). Callings are not made on the basis of acquired skills, strength of résumés, considerations of appropriate career paths, or expressed interest. Leadership assignments are not promotions to more important positions.

The Servant Leader

Contrary to popular leadership notions in many organizations today, the Lord taught that leaders are to be servants, not exalted rulers: "And whosoever shall exalt himself shall be abased; and he that shall humble himself shall be exalted" (Matthew 23:12). And, "If any man desire to be first, the same shall be last of all, and servant of all" (Mark 9:35). And, "He that is ordained of God and sent forth, the same is appointed to be the greatest, notwithstanding he is the least and the servant of all" (D&C 50:26).

Christ washed the feet of His Apostles, a task seen at His time as being below the dignity of a leader. But by so doing, He demonstrated an alternative model of leadership. The Savior taught that instead of being viewed as superior to those they lead, and often above the law, leaders should be examples of obedience to the law and see themselves as servants to rather than rulers over those they lead. "If I then, your Lord and Master, have washed your feet; ye also ought to wash one another's feet. For I have given you an example, that ye should do as I have done to you. Verily, verily, I say unto you, The servant is not greater than his lord; neither he that is sent greater than he that sent him. If ye know these things, happy are ye if ye do them" (John 13:14–17).

Why We Are Called as Church Leaders

Callings come from God, sometimes for reasons that have little to do with choosing the "strongest" candidate for a position. I have served in many Church leadership callings, for example, where I was clearly not the most qualified person in our congregation to hold that particular position—a situation that would have been considered completely inappropriate in secular organizations where I have worked.

For example, after I returned home from my mission, I went back to BYU to finish my undergraduate degree. I was honored but surprised when a high councilor called me to be a counselor in the stake Sunday School presidency. I had two major concerns. First, I felt totally unprepared to serve in a calling where part of my responsibility was to visit the wards in our stake and help evaluate the effectiveness of the teachers. Many of the teachers in our student stake were majoring in education, some at the graduate level. I had little teaching experience, no qualifications, and felt completely inadequate to help them.

My second concern was more personal. One of the members of the presidency was a brother I had known before I went to Sapporo on my mission. The nicest possible way to express my feelings about him is to say that I didn't like him. *Really* didn't like him. I won't go into the petty reasons other than to say that this brother had offended me repeatedly. I had carried this disdain around with me for years, allowing it to grow like a cancer inside of me. How could I possibly serve with him? Out of the thousands of students at BYU, why did the Lord want me to work closely with the one person I couldn't stand to be in the same room with?

I decided that I needed to pray about whether to accept the calling or not. I did, and I received a confirmation that the calling was what the Lord wanted me to do.

Thank heavens I did. Over the next several months, I learned much about Church leadership callings. For example, I learned that sometimes leadership callings are meant to benefit the leader more than those he or she serves. Unlike secular organizations where leadership positions are normally filled with those who have already demonstrated their superior competence—for example, the best engineer gets promoted to become the manager of engineering—leadership positions in the Church are often given to those who need the assignment (and the patience of those they serve) to help them become better people.

My calling helped me resolve my concerns with this other brother. I found out that he had never intended to offend me (and had no idea that he had done so). I was able to let go of the senseless burden I had been carrying around for so long. I would say that I forgave him—which is technically accurate—but in reality I came to understand that he hadn't done anything worthy of my forgiveness. How foolish I had been; how much time and energy I had wasted. The Lord knew what I needed at that point in my eternal development, and He lovingly gave me an opportunity to flush the poison of resentment from my soul and learn that taking offense where none is intended is a fool's labor.

I also learned that when I relied on the Lord that He would help me beyond my own limited abilities to perform my calling. During the dreaded teacher evaluations, for example, if I made a recommendation with humility, under the direction of the Spirit and consistent with the materials the Church had provided me, it was a wonderful learning experience for everyone involved, even when I worked with those who had far more qualifications and experience than I did. My Sunday School leadership calling taught me far more important lessons than how to administer an educational organization. To this day, I shudder to think that I almost succumbed to the temptation of declining the call.

The Lord looks at us as His younger brothers and sisters, not His employees. His leadership callings give us a chance to meet people that may become essential to our eternal progression. We learn important lessons, are put in a position where we may have unique chances to address the needs of one of our brothers or sisters and be an answer to their prayers, develop important virtues, build our testimonies, strengthen our weaknesses, learn humility, and act as a vessel of Christ's love for others.

How Church Leadership Differs from Secular Leadership

Callings differ from leadership positions in secular organizations in other ways as well (see Figure 2-1). For example, there are no rules in the Church about how we should move from calling to calling. I have been a high priest group leader three times so far—evidence, I think, that the Lord felt I needed to learn something from that particular experience that I may not yet have mastered. In many secular organizations, this repetitive practice would be viewed negatively. My wife, Mareen, has been called to be the president of the Young Women twice: once as a newly married woman too young be the mother of a Beehive and again when she was old enough to be the grandmother of the Laurels—a staffing decision that may have seemed illogical in many community organizations, but one which makes perfect sense in the Church.

Figure 2-1: Selected Differences between
Secular Organizations and the Church

Question	Many Secular Organizations	The Church
Who fills leadership positions?	Organizational leadership aided by staff members	Organizational leadership aided by inspiration
Who's ultimately responsible for leadership placement decisions?	Management	God
What factors are considered before a leader is selected?	Skill match, aptitude, previous experience, career path, availability, and so on	God's will
What is the selection process?	An opening is identified, the potential candidates submit applications, applications are screened, applicants are interviewed, a candidate is selected, and an offer is extended	An opening is identified, the potential candidates are discussed, a candidate is selected and confirmed by prayer, and a calling is extended

How long does the leader serve?	Until either the leader or the organization decides a change is needed	Until released
Why are leaders selected?	To serve the needs of the organization	To obey the will of God
What are the primary resources the leader relies on to do his or her work?	His or her own talents, skills, and energy (the arm of flesh)	Personal effort guided by inspiration

We also do not apply for or "call ourselves" to any calling. We do not quit, transfer, or "release ourselves" from any calling. Even in the callings where a pattern for length of service has been well established, there are no rules on how long we should serve—something many secular organizations would normally see as a problem.

When I was called as a bishop, for example, my stake president told me that the calling tenure was normally five years, a frequent practice then. But one of the men in our stake who served as bishop of three different wards (due to rapid growth and ward divisions) was later recalled as a bishop of the young single adult ward, making his service in the "five-year" calling last eight years. There are many famous accounts of this in earlier Church history. One of my wife's relatives, Bishop John Duncan, served as a bishop for twenty-seven years.

Other patterns of Church leadership also differ significantly from common practices in secular organizations. You could (as a friend of mine was) be the stake president one day and the ward Scoutmaster on the next; or you could be released as the stake Relief Society president to become a ward visiting teacher supervisor. You might be released from one of the Quorums of the Seventy to serve as a ward nursery leader. In secular organizations, these changes would be considered demotions, but not in the Church. We serve where and when we are needed.

Certainly all callings are different. Some take more time and effort than others; some have supervisory responsibilities. But each calling in the Church is important, regardless of its perceived status. Aside from our callings in our home (which trump every other Church assignment), there are no higher or lower callings in our wards and stakes, no more-important or less-important members. We all serve the Lord.

As the Apostle Paul so eloquently instructed, "We all [are] baptized into one body. . . . For the body is not one member, but many. If the foot shall say, Because I am not the hand, I am not of the body; is it therefore not of the body? . . . And the eye cannot say unto the hand, I have no need of thee: nor again the head to the feet, I have no need of you. Nay, much more those members of the body, which seem to be more feeble, are necessary: And those members of the body, which we think to be less honourable, upon these we bestow more abundant honour" (1 Corinthians 12:13–15, 21–23).

The inspired genius of our lay ministry is that we have no professional clergy, few specially trained or highly experienced leaders, and no elected hierarchy. No one applies or campaigns for positions. We all take our turns filling leadership assignments. We support each other. We forgive each other when leadership mistakes are made, at least partially because we know we might be the next person to serve in that exact same role.

Render unto God

Even as a twelve-year-old boy, the Savior understood that there was a significant difference between the secular world, with its way of doing things, and the kingdom of God, with its distinct way of doing things. When His frightened parents lost Him in the Jerusalem crowds, and then finally discovered Him teaching His "superiors" in the temple, they were understandably upset. But He gently explained that He was on an errand from God—an errand that required Him to do things differently than the established traditions and practices of the secular world. He would later reinforce these differences by teaching, "Render therefore unto Caesar the things which are Caesar's; and unto God the things that are God's" (Matthew 22:21).

Similarly, in Luke 16:15, He taught, "Ye are they which justify yourselves before men; but God knoweth your hearts: for that which is highly esteemed among men is abomination in the sight of God." And in Matthew, He also said, "Ye know that the princes of the Gentiles exercise dominion over them, and they that are great exercise authority upon them. But it shall not be so among you: but whosoever will be great among you, let him be your minister; and whosoever will be chief among you, let him be your servant" (Matthew 20:25–27).

Some of us who are called to leadership positions in the Church have been blessed with previous leadership experiences in schools, communities, governments, and workplaces. Many of the skills, practices, programs, and processes we have learned are transferable to Church leadership experience, and can help us better organize our stewardships and increase our efficiency and effectiveness in building the kingdom of God. But not all of the practices of Caesar—speaking broadly of all secular organizations and philosophies—are appropriate. Some, in fact, are antithetical to the work of God.

As President Ezra Taft Benson taught,

> We must remember that . . . the Church . . . is not the business world. Its success is measured in terms of souls saved, not in profit and loss. We need, of course, to be efficient and productive, but we also need to keep our focus on eternal objectives. Be cautious about imposing secular methods and terminology on sacred priesthood functions. Remember that rational problem-solving procedures, though helpful, will not be solely sufficient in the work of the kingdom. God's work must be done by faith, prayer, and by the Spirit, "and if it be by some other way it is not of God" (D&C 50:18). (*The Teachings of Ezra Taft Benson* [Salt Lake City: Bookcraft, 1988], 372–73)

Summary

Understanding how leadership callings in the Church differ from leadership positions in the secular world can help us be more effective Church leaders. Church callings are neither promotions nor demotions. Our leaders are to be servants to, not bosses over, those within their stewardships. We will learn which secular leadership skills are helpful and which are not. Understand that though we should always prepare ourselves to be worthy and capable of a Church leadership position, it is inappropriate to seek one. And though we should never campaign to be a Church leader, understand that if called, we will ultimately have an important decision to make: whether to be a Christlike leader or not.

That's probably why you're reading this book.

In the next chapter, we will learn the critical importance of setting a good example for others. If we want to emulate the core leadership competency of the Savior, we must be able, as He did, to invite those over whom we have stewardship to "come, follow me" (Luke 18:22). The unspoken sermon of personal example is far more powerful than anything we can preach from the pulpit.

CHAPTER THREE: HOW TO BE A GOOD EXAMPLE

"Be thou an example of the believers, in word, in conversation, in charity, in spirit, in faith, in purity" (1 Timothy 4:12)

fter we are called, our first assignment—often even before we understand our new leadership responsibilities—is to set a good example. In the section entitled "Leadership in the Church of Jesus Christ," *The Church Handbook of Instructions* (hereafter CHI) says, "Leaders can best teach others how to be 'true followers' by their personal example. This pattern—being a faithful disciple in order to help others become faithful disciples—is the purpose behind every calling in the Church" ("The Savior's Way of Leading," *Handbook 2: Administering the Church* [Salt Lake City: The Church of Jesus Christ of Latter-day Saints, 2010], 2:3.1).

Set a Good Example

Everything we say or do sets an example, for good or ill. So how do we set a *good* example as leaders? By doing what our Savior did. His simple admonition to "come, follow me" is the most powerful illustration of personal example in the history of leadership, even in matters where it may have seemed unnecessary. Why should He be baptized, for example, if the ordinance is for cleansing sins? He had no sins. But as we read in 2 Nephi, "And also, the voice of the Son came unto me, saying: He that is baptized in my name, to him will the

Father give the Holy Ghost, like unto me; wherefore, follow me, and do the things which ye have seen me do" (2 Nephi 31:12).

Christlike leaders don't say to people, "You should go to the temple"; they invite people to join them on an upcoming visit. They don't say, "You should keep the commandments"; they keep the commandments *even when no one is watching* because that is what they would ask of any their own leaders. They set an example of personal scripture study, church attendance, prayer, and assignment fulfillment. They don't say, "You should follow the prophet." Instead, they say, "Here's how we can work on the prophet's challenge together."

The great prophet-king Benjamin illustrated the powerful moral authority of this leadership principle when he taught,

> I, myself, have labored with mine own hands that I might serve you, and that ye should not be laden with taxes. . . . Behold, I say unto you that because I said unto you that I had spent my days in your service, I do not desire to boast, for I have only been in the service of God. And behold, I tell you these things that ye may learn wisdom; that ye may learn that when ye are in the service of your fellow beings ye are only in the service of your God. Behold, ye have called me your king; and if I, whom ye call your king, do labor to serve you, then ought not ye to labor to serve one another? (Mosiah 2:14,16–18)

My mission president often told us the story of how President Spencer W. Kimball was once the visiting Authority at a stake conference in Hawaii. President Koizumi served as the stake president and discovered at one point just prior to a meeting that President Kimball was missing. President Koizumi searched for him, eventually discovering the man he revered as a prophet, seer, and revelator in the men's restroom cleaning the floor.

Perhaps President Kimball might have chosen to give a wonderful talk in the stake conference about the importance of caring for church buildings. Perhaps he could have sent out a written communication, urging members to treat these facilities with the respect due a house of worship. But no sermon or communication would have carried that message more powerfully into the heart of President Koizumi than seeing the elderly prophet on his hands and knees in the restroom, humbly and quietly serving where service was needed.

President Thomas S. Monson is known for his similar personal righteous example. There are countless stories of his personal ministry, whether it be in a service station rescuing a priest who needed to be at church, leaving a meeting to attend to the needs of the sick, walking through the halls of a hospital to give blessings, or literally offering the less needy the clothes off his own back.

That's how the Lord did it. Of course, He taught with great power about compassion and mercy through parables and exhortation. But many of His greatest sermons were given in practice rather than in preaching. In these moments, He didn't just teach the ten lepers, those who would stone the adulteress, the parents of a dead little girl, or the Apostle who in frustration cut off the ear of an enemy. By His actions, He taught all of us who read the accounts in the scriptures.

Unlike the Savior, however, we as leaders are not perfect. Sometimes we fall short of the example we should be setting of the gospel in action. But we can set a good example in our imperfection too. Leaders who are trying to be more Christlike, for instance, are quick to apologize for their mistakes. They demonstrate genuine repentance for sins, even if the sins may seem like relatively small ones.

A Model for Christlike Leadership

We should all strive to be a "come, follow me" type of leader, as the Savior demonstrated in His personal ministry. This is the first lesson of Christlike leadership. Specifically, I'd like to suggest that we follow the Lord's example in seven important areas that leadership experts call "competencies" (see Figure 3-1).

Figure 3-1: The Christlike Leader

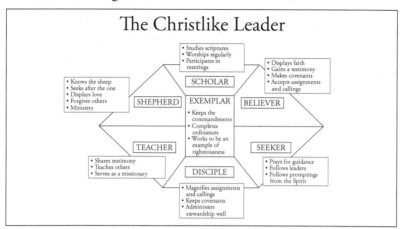

Though understanding how He led during his mortal sojourn will not enable us to demonstrate a similar perfection in our own leadership callings, it can definitely help us improve our efforts to set a more Christlike example. As we discuss the competencies, we will also review the attributes commonly associated with Christ: virtue, temperance, godliness, knowledge, faith, hope, humility, obedience, diligence, courage, patience, charity, and brotherly kindness (see Figure 3-2).

Now, let's examine each competency in more detail.

Exemplar

I believe that the core competency of the Savior's earthly ministry was to be an exemplar, as we have already discussed. How glorious it would be if all Church leaders could honestly say, as the Savior did, "For I have given you an example, that ye should do as I have done to you" (John 13:15). And, "Therefore, what manner of men ought ye to be? Verily I say unto you, even as I am" (3 Nephi 27:27).

A Church leader strives to be a good example, especially when it comes to keeping the commandments. As Paul taught, "The Lord ordained that they which preach the gospel should live of the gospel" (1 Corinthians 9:14).

An exemplar is righteous. He or she completes all of the necessary ordinances and strives to emulate the Christlike attributes appropriate to this competency: virtue, temperance, and godliness.

Scholar

The Lord also demonstrated the importance of being a gospel scholar. He often quoted scripture, for example, as He taught those who followed Him. And He gently criticized those who served as religious leaders who did not know or understand the writings of the prophets: "And Jesus answering said unto them, Do ye not therefore err, because ye know not the scriptures, neither the power of God?" (Mark 12:24).

His practice of regular scripture study, church attendance, and personal devotion began early in His life and became a regular habit, as indicated in Luke: "And he came to Nazareth, where he had been brought up: and, *as his custom was*, he went into the synagogue on the sabbath day, and stood up for to read" (Luke 4:16; emphasis added).

The Christlike attribute associated with this competency is knowledge, and the Christlike leader develops this knowledge by setting a personal example of regular scripture study, church attendance, and active participation in all the gospel knowledge–enhancing opportunities available, including our Sunday services such as the sacrament, Sunday School, and priesthood or Relief Society meetings; weekday activities; seminary or institute; training meetings; and regular temple worship.

Believer

The Savior was able to help others believe because He too was a believer. He taught the gospel from His deep personal reservoir of faith and hope—the attributes associated with this competency. The scriptures teach that His faith was strong and began early in His life. "And the child grew, and waxed strong in spirit, filled with wisdom: and the grace of God was upon him" (Luke 2:40).

With this faith, He performed mighty miracles and gave others the hope that there was a God who loved them, a life after death, and a freedom from the travails and oppression of mortal existence. Similarly, the Christlike leader gains a testimony and displays his or her faith by doing things such as making covenants and accepting assignments and callings.

Seeker

Remarkably, even our Savior, the greatest of us all, displayed the humility necessary to seek out the will of the Father. Regardless of His own perfection—or perhaps better stated as *because* of His own perfection—He continuously sought divine guidance: "I seek not mine own will, but the will of the Father which hath sent me" (John 5:30).

Even in His darkest moment in Gethsemane, when Christ wanted to let the cup pass from Him, He ended His prayer with the same three words He taught His disciples to use in their prayers: "Thy will be done" (Matthew 26:42). The Christlike leader prays for similar guidance, follows inspired leaders, and seeks out and follows the promptings of the Spirit.

Disciple

The Lord was a perfect example of discipleship. "I do nothing of myself; but as my Father hath taught me, I speak these things" (John 8:28). And, "For I came down from heaven, not to do mine own will, but the will of him that sent me" (John 6:38). The attributes He showed as a disciple were obedience and diligence, attributes the Christlike leader displays as he or she magnifies his or her calling and assignments, keeps covenants, and learns to properly administer the stewardship the Lord has given him or her.

As President N. Eldon Tanner explained, "Some people fail to become great leaders because they have not learned to follow instructions—even the teachings of Jesus Christ. In order, then, to lead as Jesus led, we must first learn to follow Christ as he followed his Father in heaven" ("Leading As the Savior Led," *Liahona*, January 1978).

Teacher

Much of the record we have of the Lord's life contains the content and method of his miraculous teaching. He taught as one having authority, unlike the Pharisees and Sadducees of His day, and He used powerful techniques that Christlike leaders emulate. His teachings were rarely critical—mostly loving in tone. He used questions to make people think and parables to adapt gospel messages to the lives and understanding of the learners. As a teacher, He demonstrated the attributes of courage and patience. He took personal risks and wasn't afraid of how others might view him. So must we, as modern leaders, share our testimonies often, teach at every appropriate opportunity, and serve continuously as missionaries of the Savior.

One of my favorite stories about the Lord's teachings was when He is only twelve years old. We read of this experience: "And it came to pass, that after three days they found him in the temple, sitting in the midst of the doctors, both hearing them, and asking them questions. And all that heard him were astonished at his understanding and answers" (Luke 2:46–47). He displayed this remarkable teaching skill all of His days.

Shepherd

One of the greatest competencies of Christlike leadership can be described as shepherding. The Savior is the good shepherd, the One who knows the names of the sheep and is known of them—He who would forsake the many to serve the one. His ministry of charity and brotherly kindness is an example to all. Paul encourages us to "walk in love, as Christ also hath loved us, and hath given himself for us an offering and a sacrifice to God" (Ephesians 5:2).

A Christlike leader strives to follow the Lord's example by getting to know those he or she serves, spending time in their homes, searching out those who need to be rescued, displaying love, forgiving others, and ministering to the needs of the sick, the disenfranchised, and the lonely.

Figure 3-2: Christlike Attributes

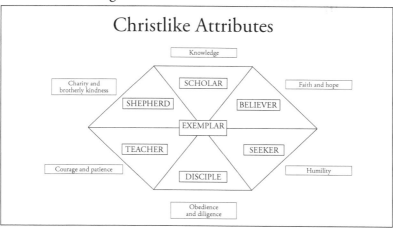

Summary

The Savior is an exemplar, scholar, believer, seeker, disciple, teacher, and shepherd. He displays divine attributes. If we want to be Christlike leaders, we must follow His admonition to do as He has done. We may never achieve perfection in our own callings as family, ward, and stake leaders, but we can certainly improve our offerings of service to Him by following His example. And to the extent that our leadership then becomes a reflected example of Him to others within our stewardship, we will be more effective in building the kingdom of God. Paul understood this when he told the Philippians, "Those things, which ye have both learned, and received, and heard, *and seen in me*, do: and the God of peace shall be with you" (Philippians 4:9; emphasis added).

The diamond-shaped figures in this chapter are called leadership models. We will refer back to them later as we begin our discussions about the more practical problems and opportunities that face Church leaders today.

In the next chapter, we'll review how to learn new roles and responsibilities after receiving a leadership calling.

CHAPTER FOUR: HOW TO LEARN NEW DUTIES AND RESPONSIBILITIES

"Wherefore, now let every man learn his duty, and to act in the office in which he is appointed, in all diligence" (D&C 107:99)

During my first year of graduate school, I found the girl of my dreams. Reenie Duncan was a raven-haired beauty in my organizational behavior program, and after repeated efforts, I finally convinced her to marry me that summer before the beginning of our second year. After we graduated together, we briefly considered doctoral studies, but opted instead to go to work in Lima, Ohio. I accepted a department management position with Procter and Gamble in a small but remarkable manufacturing plant and tried to become a corporate leader. Reenie headed up the volunteer organization of the Lima Arts Council.

Life became a tornado of activity. I struggled to learn the manufacturing and chemical technologies that the other department managers had already mastered before being promoted. I was on call all day, every day. Reenie was developing a new process for recruiting and managing community volunteers. We both worked long hours in our new careers—and we were trying to start our own family.

Just a few months after arriving, we both received callings that created a terror of anticipation. She was called as the president of the Relief Society, and I, the president of the elders quorum. Our ward was one of the largest geographical units in the Midwest, with travel time for some of our members being more than an hour each way. Traveling to the stake center was a four-hour round trip commitment. Many in the ward had serious needs.

We didn't see how we would have the time to do these callings. And we didn't have that kind of gas money. But we exhibited faith and accepted the leadership callings anyway.

We prayed to know how to do what the Lord had asked of us. We felt impressed to sell our gas guzzler and buy an inexpensive economy car, which helped. But before we could figure out how to better prioritize and manage our many time conflicts, we had to learn what was expected of us in our new callings.

Feeling Overwhelmed

These challenges can occur at any level of Church responsibility. When Kim Clark was called to be the new president of BYU–Idaho, for example, he wondered what the Brethren expected of him. President Gordon B. Hinckley declined to offer direction but suggested he discuss it with Elder David A. Bednar, who had previously shouldered the responsibility. After discussing it with Elder Bednar, Brother Clark understood why the Brethren were reluctant to be too specific in their requirements of his new assignment. Elder Bednar told him that the Lord was in charge and that he should find out through the Spirit what was expected of him, directly from that divine source (Kim B. Clark, "Leadership," *Mormon Channel Radio*, Episode 29, October 2011).

This is a common experience in the Church. Many who receive leadership callings feel overwhelmed and don't know what is expected of them. Others are driven to their knees in humility, worried their life circumstances will prevent their service. Most feel inadequate. In fact, perhaps the only people who don't feel inadequate are those who do not yet understand their new responsibilities. In any case, the appropriate step to take is that required by the Lord in D&C 107:99: "Wherefore, now let every man learn his duty, and to act in the office in which he is appointed, in all diligence."

I'd like to recommend five important resources to help us understand what is expected of us as new leaders: Church publications, current leaders, previous calling holders, the scriptures, and (most important) personal prayer. We do this so "that my people may be taught more perfectly, and have experience, and know more perfectly concerning their duty, and the things which I require at their hands" (D&C 105:10).

Church Publications (Online and Paper)

One of the blessings of modern-day revelation is that resources published by the Church in either digital or printed formats are continuously changing and improving. Reenie and I found the CHI to be an inspired repository of clear and powerful direction for anyone seeking instruction pertaining to the leadership positions covered within it (which, at the time of this writing, includes stake presidencies, high councilors, bishoprics, high priests group leadership, elders quorum presidencies, Relief Society presidencies, Young Women and Young Men leaders, Primary presidencies, Sunday School presidencies, music leaders, single member leaders, clerks, executive secretaries and many stake and ward specialists). President Ezra Taft Benson, who served not only in the senior leadership councils of the Church but also in the US government as the Secretary of Agriculture during the Eisenhower Administration, explained, "One of the best ways for leaders to understand correct principles is to have a thorough knowledge and understanding of the scriptures and the appropriate handbook. Most situations have already arisen before, perhaps many times, and policy and procedure have already been determined to handle the problem. It is always wise, therefore, to refer to and be familiar with existing written instructions and Church policy on questions as they arise" (*The Teachings of Ezra Taft Benson*, 375).

In addition to the handbooks, what a blessing it would have been to us before to have the vast online library of training materials that is now available. Many of them take only a few minutes to review, and they contain powerful instructions concerning the critical parts of most leadership callings.

The Church website (lds.org) contains outstanding training videos and instructions for most leadership callings that are as good, or better, as any I have seen in my professional career in the leadership training industry. Take advantage of them! They also include resources for teachers, family leaders, home teachers, visiting teachers, historians, auditors, and others.

Worldwide Leadership Training broadcasts are also currently available online (and accessible through many handheld devices). These training sessions by General Authorities cover issues of timely importance and carry a powerful spirit directly from our prophets, seers, and revelators. You obviously wouldn't want to miss an opportunity to attend these training meetings if they occur during your time of service. And sometimes, Church leaders travel to your areas to provide this type of instruction in person.

Be certain to search the Church website for anything online or for a reference to other resources produced by Church and approved non-Church publishers pertaining to your new calling. Though countless other wonderful resources also exist for many leadership callings through social networking websites and other publications, prayerful caution should be exercised before using any nonauthorized sources.

Current Leaders

The CHI states that certain training information should be shared with most new leaders when they are called (for example, an explanation of general responsibilities, who they report to, what meetings they will attend, and how to get resources such as physical keys or handbooks when applicable [see *Handbook 2* 2:19.2]). But I have always had many additional questions and concerns about a new leadership calling—so did my wife when she was called as Relief Society president. She had lots of specific questions, for example, about funerals, welfare orders, and visiting teaching.

After shock subsides, you might ask the leader who issues your call,

- "Why me? Why now?"
- "Who are the people that require special ministry in my new stewardship?"
- "What priorities have been identified by our ward or stake leadership?"
- "What are my responsibilities regarding [fill in the blank about specific assignments such as funerals, welfare orders, and visiting teaching]?"
- "Who can I ask questions to about how to [fill in the blank]?"

- "How do I get help if I need it?"
- "How will I know if I'm successful?"

Keep the door open with the leaders you report to so that you can continue to meet with them when necessary, but be proactive. Don't expect your leader to always come to you with direction, assignments, and clarification. If you have a question, ask. If you have an idea or proposal, share it. Remember, "For behold, it is not meet that I should command in all things; for he that is compelled in all things, the same is a slothful and not a wise servant; wherefore he receiveth no reward. . . . He that doeth not anything until he is commanded, and receiveth a commandment with doubtful heart, and keepeth it with slothfulness, the same is damned" (D&C 58:26, 29).

Strong words, but true ones. A passive leader's efforts don't flow downstream with the strength of a constant current. They may ebb, depending on the direction and energy created by others. In the absence of this encouragement, timid leaders come to a stop as surely as though a dam had prevented any forward motion.

You can be successful as a leader, even if you don't have previous leadership experience. The prophets have told us that whom the Lord calls, He qualifies. He wouldn't have called you if you couldn't be effective. You'll probably make some mistakes—we all do. Just remember to learn from them and carry on. As you keep the commandments and work hard, you will be blessed with the help you need. You are never expected to bear the burdens of leadership alone. This isn't just a job; you are helping to build the kingdom of God. And your efforts to follow the Savior's leadership example will give you both the skills and the heavenly power to do the work.

Remember this advice and testimony given to leaders by President Benson: "In the Church today a leader . . . needs to think tall. He should assure those to whom he gives assignments that in the service of the Lord they have even greater powers than in ordinary responsibilities. . . . This is His Church, His gospel plan. These are His children we are working with. He will not permit us to fail if we do our part. He will magnify us even beyond our own talents and abilities when necessary. This I know" (*The Teachings of Ezra Taft Benson*, 372).

Previous Calling Holders

This one is a little tricky. You are called to do things using your unique talents and perspectives. If the Lord wanted the previous calling holder to be doing the calling his or her way, he or she would still be doing it. Sometimes the Lord needs a fresh start in an organization. I recently heard of a mission president, for example, who was given only two hours of overlap with the previous mission president to review pressing issues. But he was specifically instructed not to talk about the missionaries. Why? Probably to allow him to develop his own untarnished opinion of the strengths and weaknesses of the elders and sisters in his new stewardship.

Nevertheless, sometimes this connection with a previous calling holder is helpful. The only person who could explain how to properly fill welfare orders to my wife, for instance, was the previous Relief Society president. When I was later called as a bishop, it was essential that I knew who was receiving counsel from the previous bishop so that I could continue ministering to them appropriately so that they wouldn't feel abandoned during the transition of leadership. The only person who knew that was the previous bishop. But don't be concerned if previous calling holders are unavailable to you. You can always use the same resource that the Lord used: the scriptures.

Scriptures

Many leadership callings are discussed directly in the scriptures. I still remember the powerful spirit I felt about the importance of teaching when I read the following passage as a new deacons quorum president: "And again, verily I say unto you, the duty of a president over the office of a deacon is to preside over twelve deacons, to sit in council with them, and to teach them their duty, edifying one another, as it is given according to the covenants" (D&C 107:85).

Responsibilities pertaining to working with children both as parents and those who work directly with Primary or young men and women are spread throughout the scriptures. Pay special attention to Moroni 8; D&C 68; 74; 93; Proverbs 22; Matthew 19; Mosiah 4; 15; 3 Nephi 22; and 17, where the Lord serves as an exemplar (the core competency in the Christlike leadership model) of how to work with younger brothers and sisters.

Christ Used Scriptures to Learn
His Leadership Responsibilities

When the young Lord told His parents in the temple that He was doing His father's business, He demonstrated a clear understanding of His personal leadership responsibility at the tender age of a latter-day deacon. We can probably assume that at least part of this understanding came from His gospel scholarship (another competency in the leadership model). We know He studied the scriptures; He frequently quoted them when He taught His followers, often using the words, "It is written."

When the Lord once returned to the synagogue of Nazareth on the Sabbath, He stood up to read and was handed the book of Esaias, which is the Greek name for the prophet we know as Isaiah:

> And when he had opened the book, he found the place where it was written, The Spirit of the Lord is upon me, because he hath anointed me to preach the gospel to the poor; he hath sent me to heal the brokenhearted, to preach deliverance to the captives, and recovering of sight to the blind, to set at liberty them that are bruised, to preach the acceptable year of the Lord. And he closed the book, and he gave it again to the minister, and sat down. And the eyes of all them that were in the synagogue were fastened on him. And he began to say unto them, This day is this scripture fulfilled in your ears. (Luke 4:17–21)

Knowing the writings of Isaiah meant Christ likely also knew the Messianic prophecies of the virgin birth (Isaiah 7:14), the long-awaited God (25:9), the Lord (40:3), and the Redeemer (59:20), who would be whipped (50:6) and wounded for our transgressions (53:5). Since we know that all of the prophets testified of Christ, He must have known other prophecies about His roles and responsibilities as well. For example, of the author of the first five books of the Old Testament (also known as the Pentateuch or Torah), He said, "For had ye believed Moses, ye would have believed me: for he wrote of me. But if ye believe not his writings, how shall ye believe my words?" (John 5:46–47).

When we search the scriptures to learn more about our callings, we are following Christ's example, who so perfectly demonstrated the competency of gospel scholarship.

Personal Prayer

Many times over the last twenty-five years, I have been speaking with a manager in a large corporation when he or she said something like this, "I'm unclear about my responsibilities pertaining to X. I wish I could just ask the senior leader directly, but I can't because [that'd be seen as breaking the chain of command, it'd be politically unwise, or I'd never be able to get an appointment]."

How fortunate we are in the Church to be able to go right to the top to get clarification and direction. If we need to understand what is expected of us, we can (and should) follow the frequent example of the Savior by praying to the Father. Christ, who had mastered the leadership competency of seeking guidance, instructed the Nephites that prayer is the key to understanding: "I perceive that ye are weak, that ye cannot understand all my words which I am commanded of the Father to speak unto you at this time. Therefore, go ye unto your homes, and ponder upon the things which I have said, and ask of the Father, in my name, that ye may understand" (3 Nephi 17:2–3).

As a competent shepherd, He then healed their sick and blessed their children. And before He left, He became an exemplar of the power of these types of personal requests for understanding and direction: "The things which he prayed cannot be written. . . . And after this manner do they bear record: The eye hath never seen, neither hath the ear heard, before, so great and marvelous things as we saw and heard Jesus speak unto the Father; and no tongue can speak, neither can there be written by any man, neither can the hearts of men conceive so great and marvelous things as we both saw and heard Jesus speak" (3 Nephi 17:15–17).

Summary

When my wife and I both received weighty leadership callings during a busy time in our early marriage, we wondered if we would be able to serve. I can't say it was easy. Much yard and housework went undone. Now, looking back, the yard and house projects seem unimportant. What we valued was growing to love those we served. We remember the blessings of somehow always having enough time to accomplish whatever was most important for our work and family. Our leadership callings were made possible because of our efforts to obtain a clearer understanding of our responsibilities. We did this by reviewing Church publications, working with our leaders and the former holders of our callings, studying the scriptures regularly, and praying a lot.

I believe that with similar effort, you will be able to come to understand what is required of you in leadership callings as well, particularly as you follow the Savior's example as a seeker of His Father's will.

In the next chapter, we will review in more detail a related challenge for many Church leaders: time management. Specifically, how do we prioritize our time and efforts to do the most good and balance the demands of our calling, work, and family responsibilities?

CHAPTER FIVE: HOW TO PRIORITIZE THROUGH VISION

"Where there is no vision, the people perish" (Proverbs 29:18)

The first time I asked for volunteers to help someone move, lots of hands shot up among the elders. I had recently been called as the elders quorum president and had been warmed with pride as I looked at the brethren around me who seemed so eager to fulfill their priesthood responsibilities.

We had a wonderful time serving together during that move, and I was thrilled to see even more hands thrust into the air when I asked the following Sunday about another moving assignment at the end of that week. But there were fewer hands for the third week's moving assignment, and the hands seemed more tentative. By the time we had our fourth assignment in four weeks, only the "faithful five"—the brethren who showed up to most activities—volunteered. Everyone else looked down when I asked for help. During our epic run of twelve moves in twelve weeks, my quorum showed signs of compassion fatigue by week five. The elders quorum presidency did the last four moves alone.

"What's wrong?" I asked my first counselor as we wrestled yet another worn couch down the outside stairs of an apartment building. "Why can't we get anybody to show up for these anymore?"

"We're an elders quorum, not a moving company," he answered. "If you keep pushing these guys, some of them might stop coming to church. They have jobs and families. Nobody has the time to do everything they would like to do. We have to find a way to prioritize."

His words stung, but they were true. I needed to manage my own personal time more effectively too. My sweetheart and I were having difficulty starting our family, and she needed more of my time than an occasional hello as we passed each other heading out to work or Church assignments.

A Vision—of Sorts

We discussed the moving problem as a presidency and prayed together for direction. We eventually felt inspired to create a different vision of how our quorum should function with moves. We imagined home teachers coordinating moves for their families and enlisting the aid of relatives and friends of the people who were moving. Then the home teacher would supplement the member's move team with a rotating set of elders. The inspired idea not only cut down the number of moves requiring more than a few additional elders, but it spread the assignments around so no one felt consistently overburdened.

We didn't have a vision in the scriptural sense of the word, but we felt grateful for what we felt was an inspired method to solve our unique problem in our highly transient ward. Envisioning an alternative approach allowed us to make better use of our time and lead the quorum to a better place.

How Vision Prioritizes Action

After two short years in Ohio, we transferred to Illinois, where I worked as an internal organizational development consultant, and Reenie joined Procter and Gamble in a separate test-market facility. We missed Lima, where we had worked so hard in the Church and made so many friends through our service. But we didn't have to wait long for new callings. The bishop called me first as an executive secretary, and then as the high priests group leader. He called Reenie as the president of the Young Women. We soon were, again, happily engaged in difficult leadership callings.

One of my very first work assignments at Procter and Gamble in Chicago was to help the plant create a long-range plan to guide our efforts over the next three to five years and provide a means for us to determine our day-to-day priorities. We had concluded that the only way for us to break through the cycle of frantic activity that kept us busy (but not as productive as we needed to be) was to carefully examine what we were doing and see if it was really leading us in the best direction or not.

As my experience in Lima with the moving problem of the elders quorum had demonstrated, I thought we might envision a better alternative to the way we were doing things in the failing plant and put together a plan to reach that vision. Surprisingly, the factory managers and union officers who participated in the planning effort readily accepted the idea.

It has always amazed me that the analytical and often cynical business world so easily accepts the concept of "vision" from the religious world. But I probably shouldn't be surprised. The idea of vision-led leadership is an incredibly motivating force. When people feel that their leader has a vision of a desirable future, they are much more likely to follow him or her. No one likes to dance to an uncertain beat. What business leaders miss from the religious view of vision is that when that vision comes from God, the leader is entitled to divine assistance in the accomplishment of the vision as well.

The Visionary Leader

Our scriptures are full of these powerful examples of visionary leaders. The Restoration of the gospel began with what we refer to as the First Vision. Though Joseph was ridiculed for speaking of his vision, he courageously declared, "Though I was hated and persecuted for saying that I had seen a vision, yet it was true . . . I have actually seen a vision; and who am I that I can withstand God, or why does the world think to make me deny what I have actually seen?" (Joseph Smith—History 1:25). Bolstered with the courage and conviction that came from the vision (and subsequent visions and instructions that followed), Joseph restored the Lord's Church.

Many ancient Church leaders also had visions, which they used as a tool of leadership. To mention only a few: Isaiah (Isaiah 2: latter-day temples, gathering of Israel, the Second Coming), Ezekiel (Ezekiel 40: the location and design of the temple), Joseph (2 Nephi 3: the Nephites and Joseph Smith), Zacharias (Luke 1: he and Elizabeth would have a son named John), Peter (Acts 10: taking the gospel to the Gentiles), Paul (Acts 16: to preach in Macedonia), John (Revelation 9: wars and plagues preceding the Second Coming), and Amulek (Alma 8: he should feed Alma). Some of these visions came to prophets to clarify doctrine or action for the entire Church, others provided direction for a subset of the Church, and still others were for the guidance of a single person or family.

Let's consider the prophet Lehi in more detail, to better understand how vision can be an effective tool for leading and prioritizing. Lehi's own family members called him a visionary man—they didn't always mean that as a compliment. Even the valiant Sariah, Lehi's wife, complained when she incorrectly assumed that her sons had been killed when Lehi sent them off to get the plates of Laban:

> For she had supposed that we had perished in the wilderness; and she also had complained against my father, telling him that he was a visionary man. . . . And it had come to pass that my father spake unto her, saying: I know that I am a visionary man; for if I had not seen the things of God in a vision I should not have known the goodness of God, but had tarried at Jerusalem, and had perished with my brethren. But behold, I have obtained a land of promise . . . yea, and I know that the Lord will deliver my sons out of the hands of Laban, and bring them down again unto us in the wilderness. (1 Nephi 5:2, 4–5)

One of Lehi's visions showed the destruction of Jerusalem and led him to preach repentance. He likely had many responsibilities in his business and community. (We know, for example, that his labors had allowed him to amass enough wealth to make Laban envious.) But his vision caused him to reprioritize his focus, culminating in an evacuation of his family from Jerusalem and an abandonment of his worldly riches. When the Lord instructed Lehi to begin the journey to the land of promise, He also blessed them with the Liahona the next morning—a compass dependent on their faith and diligence—to show them how to get to Lehi's envisioned destination.

In the April 1990 general conference, Elder Spencer J. Condie spoke about the vision of Lehi's son Nephi, and about why vision is so important to us as leaders:

> From the Book of Mormon we read of the young prophet Nephi who also beheld a vision on a mountain. Once he had envisioned the

1 Nephi 3:7

promised land, he could not be dissuaded from building a ship that would take him there. Once parents have a vision of a son dressed in a missionary suit or of a daughter in the temple dressed in white, then family home evening, family prayer, and scripture study assume their proper place in every home. From Moses and Nephi we learn that a leader must have a vision of the work which lies ahead. ("Some Scriptural Lessons on Leadership," *Ensign*, May 1990)

Key Elements of a Vision

Through vision, leaders identify specific opportunities for significant improvement. Brigham Young, for example, led the Saints westward to the promised land of his vision, much like how Lehi led his family away from Jerusalem. A high priests group leader might lead ward members to the temple after receiving a prompting, which is a type of personal vision. Though, in this example, the leader may not have seen an angel or had a special dream, the effect of his personal vision on his followers can be just as clear and powerful as though he had.

Usually, the vision of a Church leader doesn't help people move from one geographical spot to another, but rather from one state of being to another: from pride to humility, selfishness to service, or misery to happiness, for example. Leaders invite people to leave their own personal Jerusalem or Sodom or Nauvoo to journey to the land of promise, where they can become converted and desire to do good continually.

Regardless of the type of journey, a visionary leader helps his followers identify three key things, as illustrated in Lehi's story. First, people must know the envisioned destination (such as Zion, the temple, or improved home teaching). Second, they must understand where they are at now (Nauvoo, unendowed, less effective in home teaching than their capability allows, and so on). Third, they must understand how to get from here to there (for example, the Oregon Trail, using the Liahona, or striving to complete one month of 100 percent home teaching).

After the vision is shared, prioritization can happen on many levels. The activities that are contrary to the vision should be eliminated. The things we are doing that help us accomplish the mission should be maintained. Then we can decide which of our activities are more useful to the accomplishment of the vision and which are less useful. I like a method for prioritizing our efforts shared by Elder Dallin H. Oaks in his conference talk entitled "Good, Better, Best" in the October 2007 general conference. If we categorize our efforts into "good, better, [and] best," we can focus on the best things and forego some of the time-consuming, less-effective good ones.

The visioning process appears to have a sequence. Leaders who start with the envisioned destination (third column) in the following Figure 5-1 are able to trim down the second column (via which pathways) to only the most critical items. Less visionary leaders, however, generally start with the second column without much focus on the third one. This often creates a proliferation of activities, meetings, and programs that, while often good, are not the best use of time for either the leader or those within his or her stewardship. As a rule of thumb, the visionary leader will only add activities that are motivated by a clearly inspired vision that benefits the brothers or sisters he or she serves (and builds the kingdom of God) and are appropriate to the starting place clarified in column one (current location). A less visionary leader tends to treat activities as an end in and of themselves.

Figure 5-1: Selected Examples of Visionary Leadership

From Current Location (Step Two)	Via Which Pathways (Step Three)	To Envisioned Destination (Step One)
Jerusalem	Use the Liahona, build boat, get plates from Laban, bring Ishmael and his daughters, and bring seeds and tents and supplies (but don't worry about taking Lehi's wealth)	The land of promise

People not going to the temple enough	Do sacrament talks on the importance of the temple, have executive secretary contact people for recommend interviews one month prior to expiration, teach family history class to motivate people to bring their own names, and encourage temple attendance during tithing settlements	Increased temple attendance
Helping people move in the way we have always done it	Assign home teachers to coordinate moves (and don't do it like we used to), use friends and relatives of person moving, and rotate a list of available elders to supplement move team	Serving people in a way that is sustainable

What Are Good Visions?

The CHI provides excellent guidance on the types of visions that leaders should consider to guide their efforts and provide direction to those within their stewardship:

Families: Teach the preeminence of the home and family as the basic organizational unit of the Church. . . . *Adults:* Encourage each adult to be worthy to receive the ordinances of the temple. . . . *Youth:* Help prepare each young man to receive the Melchizedek Priesthood, to receive the ordinances of the temple, and to be worthy to serve a full-time mission. Help prepare each young woman to be worthy to make and keep sacred covenants and receive the ordinances of the temple. ("Leadership Purposes," *Handbook 2: Administering the Church*, 3.4)

Vision Statements

Later in my life, I was called to be a counselor in a stake presidency. When (then) Elder Dieter F. Uchtdorf of the Quorum of the Twelve called our stake president, he suggested that our president create a vision statement—a document that clarified the general purpose and direction of our stake. Our president invited the high councilors and bishops to submit ideas and scriptures that would aid in the creation of a document. After much discussion and prayer, a one-page document was created and distributed throughout the stake that clarified key stake priorities in "bringing people to Christ." This document served for years as an aid to determining our direction and prioritizing our initiatives.

I have seen this idea applied elsewhere as well. There are several families in our stake, for example, who have created similar documents. Some call them family vision statements, and others call them mission statements. They often include phrases such as *our home will be a place of love and refuge from the world; we are children of God who love him and keep his commandments; we believe in wholesome family recreation—preferably on water; we eat, pray, and laugh together; or families are forever.*

These documents can help prioritize the often overcrowded schedule of a typical LDS family by simply providing an excuse for any family member to ask: Is the activity we are considering consistent with our vision or not? If not, it is eliminated. This is an ancient idea that goes back at least as far as the prophet Joshua, who shared his family's vision statement when he declared, "As for me and my house, we will serve the Lord" (Joshua 24:15).

Even our Heavenly Father has a vision statement that provides ongoing direction for His work with His children: "This is my work and my glory—to bring to pass the immortality and eternal life of man" (Moses 1:39).

The Savior as a Visionary Leader

No one, of course, was better at visionary leadership than the Savior. But though He certainly had visions (see Matthew 4:11; 17:1–9), I cannot find any scriptural evidence of Him speaking publicly about those visions during His mortal probation. In fact, He warned those who witnessed the theophany at the Mount of Transfiguration to keep it confidential: "And as they came down from the mountain, Jesus charged them, saying, Tell the vision to no man, until the Son of man be risen again from the dead" (Matthew 17:9).

Perhaps these manifestations were too sacred to discuss; there were probably other reasons for why they weren't mentioned to others as well. I wonder if one reason was that it was unnecessary for the Lord to do it. He was visionary *without* referencing His dramatic visitations from the other side of the veil. By referring only to the type of revelation that is available to all of us through personal prayer, He still painted a picture of an envisioned future of the kingdom of God that was so powerful and vivid that the ruling religious and political figures of His time found Him personally threatening.

When He taught about the good Samaritan, the generous widow, or the wise father of the prodigal son, for example, we too are inspired to become our better selves and move from our current states as sinners to something better. He didn't have to tell us that He had learned these truths in vision. Did the Lord lead this way to set an example for us as future leaders, to show us how to be visionary without requiring dramatic angelic manifestations?

Most of us will never have the sort of visions that are recorded in both ancient and modern scripture. But by following the example of the Lord, we can still be visionary leaders who prioritize our time and the time of those we lead effectively. Simple, quiet, personal revelation—not angelic ministrations—is the critical component for a personal vision to help those we lead. The Savior showed us that.

We are warned against seeking signs. And we know from the experience of Lehi's children Laman and Lemuel—who saw angels but still rebelled—that these divine manifestations do not convert anyway. Sometimes they can do worse. When a few of the Brethren assumed they needed to have the same kinds of visions as Joseph Smith to perform their priesthood duties, they received visions generated from the wrong source. We read in D&C 50: "Behold, verily I say unto you, that there are many spirits which are false spirits, which have gone forth in the earth, deceiving the world. And also Satan hath sought to deceive you, that he might overthrow you" (D&C 50:2–3).

Summary

Even though there are some who will receive visions like those of Lehi and other great prophets, these dramatic spiritual manifestations are rare and unrequired for us to be visionary leaders. Personal revelation is the key to leadership, not whether we have seen angels. We learn this from the Lord's personal example. He received visions but didn't use them as a tool of His leadership.

As visionary leaders we can move the work of the Lord forward by helping those within our stewardships understand how to live better lives. We do this by helping them understand where they are, what it looks like to be somewhere better, and how to get from here to there. This type of vision is not only an effective tool of leadership but also an excellent method for prioritizing the flood of activities that are often drowning members of the Church (leaders and followers alike).

In the next chapter, we will review in more detail how to receive personal revelation—the key to visionary leadership.

CHAPTER SIX: HOW TO RECEIVE REVELATION

"If thou shalt ask, thou shalt receive revelation upon revelation, knowledge upon knowledge, that thou mayest know the mysteries and peaceable things—that which bringeth joy, that which bringeth life eternal" (D&C 42:61)

While we were in Chicago, Reenie and I began having some new leadership experiences. Reenie became so close to the young women she had been called to serve that she loved them like daughters—the daughters, our doctors told us, that we might not ever be able to have on our own. She prayed for them by name almost daily and fasted for them when they had troubles. The Lord blessed her with insights into the hearts of these wonderful young women and through revelation allowed her to tailor the activities of the organization she led to better meet their individual needs. She visited them in their homes on their birthdays and when they were ill or sad. And they congregated in our little home often, spilling out of our nine-hundred-square-foot-cottage like gold bursting the seams of a cramped treasure chest. I write this chapter thirty years later, and Reenie (currently serving for the second time as the president of the Young Women) is still corresponding with four of "our Chicago girls."

We learned much about revelation in those two years of service. She received revelation about how to include a shy girl, touch the heart of a less-active one, and adapt the program to someone more interested in the arts than preparing for marriage and motherhood. This was before the Young Women organization had advisors, and she spent much of her time without two counselors. But I don't believe she missed a birthday or special occasion, despite working with a large group of young women while she was working full-time and commuting at least an hour each way into the city every weekday.

Only the foolhardy attempt to complete leadership callings in the Church without divine assistance. It is, in fact, a sign of arrogance to do so. The Lord has instructed, "And if any man shall seek to build up himself, and seeketh not my counsel, he shall have no power, and his folly shall be made manifest" (D&C 136:19).

The Revelatory Process

I learned much from my sweetheart during those times about both the need for and the process of revelation. I used what I learned from her in my calling as high priests group leader, and I depended on it later when I served as a bishop. In fact, one of my greatest joys about serving as the president of the Aaronic Priesthood was sitting down with newly called class or quorum presidents. I would challenge them to pray about whom to recommend as counselors, and then teach them about the revelatory process. We would read D&C 9:7–9 together: "Behold, you have not understood; you have supposed that I would give it unto you, when you took no thought save it was to ask me. But, behold, I say unto you, that you must study it out in your mind; then you must ask me if it be right, and if it is right I will cause that your bosom shall burn within you; therefore, you shall feel that it is right. But if it be not right you shall have no such feelings, but you shall have a stupor of thought that shall cause you to forget the thing which is wrong."

I would ask, "What do you think it means where it says you 'took no thought but to ask me'?" The newly called youth leaders often weren't sure.

Then I'd ask, "Well, do you think it's okay to just pray, 'Heavenly Father, please tell me who my counselors should be'?"

"Guess not," most of them then replied.

"So what do you have to do?"

"It says I have to study it out in my mind."

"How do you do that?"

"I have to decide who I think would be the best counselors."

"That's right. And then you wait for a confirmation. How will you know if the answer is yes?"

"It says my bosom will burn."

"Do you know what that means?"

"Not really."

"Have you ever felt the Spirit before?" I usually at this point would mention an event where I thought the young leader may have felt the Spirit—for example, at a testimony meeting during girls' camp, at seminary, at the temple doing baptisms for the dead, or at a bishop's youth discussion at my home a few Sunday evenings ago where I saw them wipe away tears.

To my delight, most of them would answer, "Yes." I often assume that was one of the primary reasons the Lord inspired us to call them as leaders. That way, they would be able to help other youth within their stewardships also learn to identify the Spirit.

"Tell me how the Spirit felt to you."

Most of the youth would say things such as, "It felt good [or warm, calm, peaceful]."

"Can you see how someone might describe that feeling as being like a fire inside of them?"

To the youth who hadn't felt the Spirit—or had felt it but not yet recognized it as the Spirit—I would say something like, "Well, the Spirit makes me feel peaceful. It's a warm, comforting feeling inside my heart and mind. It makes me feel like my Heavenly Father loves me, and that everything will be okay. I felt it when I prayed to get a testimony of the Book of Mormon when I was in college. I feel it in the temple and in many meetings. I think that's what a burning in the bosom means." Then I would say, "That warm feeling is what you will feel if the answer is yes. If the answer is no, what will you feel?"

"It says a 'stupor of thought.'"

"Do you know what that is?"

"No."

"Well, you won't feel the Spirit. You would feel confused, maybe even sometimes forgetful. Do you think you can tell the difference between 'the burning in the bosom' and the 'stupor of thought? Will you give it a try and call me when you have the names of your proposed counselors?"

"Okay, Bishop."

I still feel a little tender when I think about having this conversation more than thirty times in five and a half years because every single time I asked new presidents or first assistants whether they had received confirming revelation about the names they were proposing to me, they answered yes.

This is the revelation spoken of in 2 Nephi 28:30: "For behold, thus saith the Lord God: I will give unto the children of men line upon line, precept upon precept, here a little and there a little; and blessed are those who hearken unto my precepts, and lend an ear unto my counsel, for they shall learn wisdom."

Revelation about Revelation

Leaders do well to remember that Church members also can and should seek to know for themselves whether their leaders are receiving and acting on revelation or not. In warning of blind obedience, Brigham Young said, "I am more afraid that this people have so much confidence in their leaders that they will not inquire for themselves of God whether they are led by him. I am fearful they settle down in a state of blind self security. Let every man and woman know, by the whispering of the Spirit of God to themselves, whether their leaders are walking in the path the Lord dictates, or not" (John A. Widtsoe, *Discourses of Brigham Young* [Salt Lake City, Utah: Deseret Book, 1954], 135).

Christ's Example of Receiving Revelation

As you would expect, the Savior again sets a perfect example of seeking and receiving revelation (one of His key leadership competencies we've already discussed). He was often on His knees seeking the will of His Father, that He might be obedient: "I am Jesus Christ; I came by the will of the Father, and I do his will" (D&C 19:24).

We read of the specific revelatory process we have been reviewing in Luke's account of calling the Twelve Apostles, illustrating that the Savior sought the Father's will about who should serve. "And it came to pass in those days, that he went out into a mountain to pray, and continued all night in prayer to God. And when it was day, he called unto him his disciples: and of them he chose twelve, whom also he named apostles" (Luke 6:12–13).

To follow the will of the Father, of course, the Son had to have the Father's will revealed to Him. But He didn't get all the revelation He needed at once. Similarly, we as leaders have opportunities to receive direction through revelation, here a little and there a little, following the pattern established by Christ as He prepared for His ministry. This was noted in the writings of John: "And I, John, bear record that I beheld his glory, as the glory of the Only Begotten of the Father, full of grace and truth, even the Spirit of truth, which came and dwelt in the flesh, and dwelt among us. And I, John, saw that he received not of the fulness at the first, but received grace for grace" (D&C 93:11–12).

Consider the following illuminating personal example by President Joseph F. Smith: "When I as a boy first started out in the ministry, I would frequently go out and ask the Lord to show me some marvelous thing, in order that I might receive a testimony. But the Lord withheld marvels from me, and showed me the truth, line upon line, precept upon precept, here a little and there a little, until he made me to know the truth from the crown of my head to the soles of my feet, and until doubt and fear had been absolutely purged from me. He did not have to send an angel from the heavens to do this, nor did he have to speak with the trump of an archangel" (Joseph F. Smith, *Gospel Doctrine*, 11th edition [Salt Lake City: Deseret Book, 1959], 7).

Warnings about Revelation

It is a magnificent blessing to receive revelation for our families, our callings, and ourselves. But the Lord cautioned, "For although a man may have many revelations, and have power to do many mighty works, yet if he boasts in his own strength, and sets at naught the counsels of God, and follows after the dictates of his own will and carnal desires, he must fall and incur the vengeance of a just God upon him" (D&C 3:4).

During our time in Chicago, we had a sobering experience. A family in our ward claimed to be receiving revelation that went beyond their stewardship. This is never appropriate, and it caused some serious problems. During the early days of the Church, when many of the administrative precepts were still being given line upon line, well-intended members took it upon themselves to receive revelation for the stewardships of others, including (in some extreme cases) the Church as a whole. But the Lord said, "I have appointed unto my servant Joseph to hold this power in the last days, and there is never but one on the earth at a time on whom this power and the keys of this priesthood are conferred. . . . Behold, mine house is a house of order, saith the Lord God, and not a house of confusion" (D&C 132:7–8). We see a similar proclamation in section 43:2.

The Revealed Organization of the Church

Though we are entitled to leadership revelations for our families, our stewardships, and ourselves, we are not entitled to revelation for others outside our stewardships.

The Lord's Church has been compared to a body, with Christ at the head: "Christ is the head of the church: and he is the saviour of the body" (Ephesians 5:23). Also, "And he is the head of the body, the church: who is the beginning, the firstborn from the dead; that in all things he might have the preeminence" (Colossians 1:18).

Obviously the body takes direction from the head; chaos would ensue if it were otherwise. Revelations for the whole Church go to the First Presidency, who form a quorum of three presiding high priests of the Melchizedek Priesthood mentioned in D&C 107:22—the president of which is to "preside over the whole church, and be like unto Moses" (verse 91).

Twelve Apostles form a presiding quorum of special witnesses of Christ (verse 23). This follows the pattern established by Christ, who called Apostles to teach the Church during the meridian of time. He also called the Quorum of Seventy, as we read in Luke 10:1.

The Seventy have seven presiding presidents (verse 93), with one president presiding over the other six (verse 94), who may each preside over an additional seventy "until seven times seventy, if the labor in the vineyard of necessity requires it" (verse 96).

While the leadership councils of the Church have presiding authority as cited above, one is not superior to another, as follows: "[The Twelve Apostles] form a quorum, equal in authority and power to the [First Presidency] previously mentioned" (verse 24). And, "[The Seventy] form a quorum, equal in authority to that of the Twelve special witnesses or Apostles just named" (verse 26).

The structure of the stakes of Zion mirror those at the head of the Church, where there is a "quorum of the presidency" known as a stake or district presidency and standing "high councils" consisting of twelve high councilors (verse 36). Each stake or district is then divided into wards or branches, presided over by a bishopric (verse 15), with a bishop (verse 69) or branch president. Within these wards or branches are divisions into auxiliaries and levels of priesthood (D&C 107:60–75, 85–89).

Interestingly, much of this revelation was delivered on May 3, 1835. Just a few years earlier, in July of 1831, the *Niles Weekly Register* of Baltimore estimated the entire membership of the Church to be only about a thousand souls (*Niles Weekly Register*, July 6, 1891, Volume XLI—the newsweekly had arguably the largest circulation in the United States and was widely regarded as the *New York Times* or *Washington Post* of its day). At this time, there were not enough members to fill all of the leadership, but the prophetic organization given to Joseph Smith is unparalleled even today. As a consultant to many Fortune 100 companies and government agencies on matters of leadership and corporate structure, I find the clarity, flexibility, scalability (ability to scale up or down as the numbers change), efficiency, and effectiveness of this inspired structure without peer.

Limitations on Revelation

Why all of the discussion about the leadership structure of the Church? Only to demonstrate that reaching for revelation outside of the sphere of our stewardships is inappropriate. We should seek for and discuss only that revelation pertaining to our current callings. A stake president is not entitled to revelation for the whole Church, nor is a president of the Young Men entitled to revelation for a ward. Similarly, a bishop will not receive revelation for a ward other than his own, nor for the next bishop of his own ward. Elders quorum presidents don't receive revelation for the Young Women organization, nor the Relief Society president for the Young Men and so forth.

Even a faithful man who has previously had great responsibility in one of the Quorums of the Seventy will not receive revelation about how a less-active single mother on his street should lead her family. She alone is entitled to that revelation. A high priests group leader will not receive revelation for the deacons quorum in his ward, even if the deacons quorum president is his son—which brings us to the importance of keys.

Priesthood Keys

After I was called as a counselor in a stake presidency, my wife and I had a wonderful opportunity to receive special training for leaders of young men at the BSA Philmont Ranch in New Mexico. Members of the Young Men general and Primary general presidencies of the Church instructed us to respect priesthood keys, regardless of the age of the key holder with a metaphor that I will always remember. "Brethren," several of them instructed repeatedly, "stop pushing the truck! Let the ones with the keys get in and drive it."

As you know from your temple recommend interviews, we sustain the president of The Church of Jesus Christ of Latter-day Saints as a prophet, seer, and revelator, and as the only person on earth who possesses and is authorized to exercise all priesthood keys. These keys include the right to preside over and direct an appointed stewardship and are delegated by the prophet to certain priesthood leaders for the duration of their callings. The Twelve Apostles and the presidency of the Seventy also hold special priesthood keys. Keys are delegated from the prophet to presidents of temples, missions, stakes, districts, and branches. And while it is never a good idea to get in the way of any Church leader's opportunity of receiving appropriate revelation for his or her stewardship, it is especially problematic to circumvent the revelatory rights of a key holder. A wise president of the Young Men who is counseling with a deacons or teachers quorum president, for example, says, "President, my counsel to you is to exercise your keys and pray about what should be done in your quorum"—not, "Here's what I think you should do."

Don't push the truck.

While Elder Paul D. M. Christensen was visiting our stake conference in 2013 as an Area Seventy, he demonstrated this point during our priesthood leadership meeting by having someone role-play a new deacons quorum president while he played the role of the adult advisor. The roleplay went something like this:

Advisor: "President, I'm your advisor, how would you like me to advise you?"

Deacons quorum president: "I dunno."

Advisor: "How about we turn to Doctrine and Covenants section 20 and find out what deacons are supposed to do."

President: "Okay."

Advisor: "What does it say in verse 59?"

President: "We're supposed to warn, expound, exhort, teach, and invite all to come unto Christ."

Advisor: "Do you know how to do that?"

President: "No."

Advisor: "How would you like me to advise you?"

President: "I'm not sure. Maybe you can give me a chance to teach with you. Can I think about it?"

Advisor: "Of course. Why don't you pray about it too, and we'll talk next week."

Notice that the advisor advised without taking over. He helped the key holder retain his divinely appointed responsibility.

Praying Properly for Revelation

When I was serving my second time as a high councilor, I had an interesting experience with personal revelation. I was charged by the stake presidency to recommend someone for a stake calling within my stewardship and, after approval, issue the calling. As I recall, in my prayers concerning this assignment, I shared the name I felt good about and asked, "Is this the man who should be the new [name of calling]." I felt the confirmation of the Spirit, discussed that name with the bishop, received approval to proceed from the stake presidency, and set an appointment to issue the call.

When the brother arrived at the stake center, I could tell something was wrong. And as I began the interview, he stopped me and explained that he was unworthy to serve. I ended the meeting and encouraged him to contact his bishop as quickly as possible.

The experience troubled me for several weeks. I wondered why I had felt a confirmation to call someone who was unable to serve.

A few days later, the brother saw me in the hallway at church. Beaming, he expressed appreciation for our meeting and told me he had gone to the bishop and was now in the process of lifting the weight of sin off his shoulders. "I never would have gone to the bishop if it wasn't for that meeting," he said.

The answer to my prayers for understanding became clear. Heavenly Father wanted me to meet with the brother. That was the direction I received from the Spirit, but it had little to do with a calling. Heavenly Father was far more interested in having one of His sons receive the blessings of the Atonement than He was in having me complete a stake staffing assignment. He had answered my prayer in the way that was necessary to fulfill His greater purpose.

At that moment, I also felt directed by the Spirit that I had not prayed properly. Instead of praying whether someone should be the next this or that calling, I understood that I should pray about whether I should propose that someone have a calling extended to them or not. This seemingly small wording change is important for three reasons. First, it doesn't contradict agency. Asking, in effect, who will accept a calling isn't necessary for us to know. That is theirs to decide. Second, it allows whoever has the keys to approve a staffing recommendation to use their revelatory rights to disapprove the recommendation for reasons that are sometimes inappropriate to share with the person who made the recommendation. Third, it allows the Lord to inspire us to meet with people under the auspices of a calling that may have a greater need for the meeting than a calling alone.

I know of a sister, for example, who declined a calling, but because an inspired stake president felt prompted to give her a blessing, she broke down in tears of gratitude for the witness she received (and had been praying for) that Father in Heaven loved her. I know of at least two cases where a bishop exercised his keys and declined a recommendation for a calling suggested by a ward leader but then felt prompted to meet with that member anyway and thereby uncovered serious spiritual or financial needs that required immediate action. I also know of a case where a man declined a calling but then became motivated because of that meeting to change his job so that he could spend more time with his family and accept similar callings in the future.

I believe that each of these incidents were revealed for important reasons benefitting the person for whom the revelation was given. But ironically, the leaders thought they had failed in their revelatory responsibilities, sometimes in the moment when their revelation had been a tipping point in someone's eternal progression.

Summary

One of the greatest blessings a Church leader has is the opportunity to receive divine guidance for his or her calling through revelation. But overreaching for revelation can cause serious problems. A wise leader understands what revelations he or she is entitled to and learns how to pray for them properly.

In the next chapter, we will discuss how to magnify your leadership calling in more detail.

CHAPTER SEVEN: HOW TO MAGNIFY YOUR CALLING

"For whoso is faithful unto the obtaining these two priesthoods of which I have spoken, and the magnifying their calling, are sanctified by the Spirit unto the renewing of their bodies" (D&C 84:33)

*O*ne of my favorite responsibilities in the stake presidency is interviewing brethren who are being considered for advancement to or within the Melchizedek Priesthood. We always read the oath and covenant of the priesthood found in Doctrine and Covenants section 84 together, and I ask, "What do you think it means to magnify your calling?" After we talk, I try to have the candidate consider applying these ideas to a specific calling. "Tell me," I say, "how does someone who magnifies his calling as a home teacher act differently than someone who does not?" One of the most interesting answers I've ever received was, "He goes twice a month instead of once a month."

Magnifying Doesn't Mean Expanding

I think this answer demonstrates a common but, I believe, incorrect understanding of what it means to magnify a calling. Perhaps the misunderstanding comes from thinking about how a magnifying glass—a common contemporary use of this word—makes something being observed seem bigger.

What is the problem with this misunderstanding? An extended family member, while serving as a bishop, explained it to me this way: "The worst thing that can happen to a ward is to have somebody in the stake magnify their calling." He was speaking, of course, of those well-intended few who think that unless they expand the number or duration of meetings and activities that they aren't fulfilling their leadership responsibilities. Others enlarge the scope of their responsibilities to include assignments or authority that goes beyond what is in the CHI, or they usurp the responsibilities of others. The worst case is when someone inflates the importance of his or her calling.

As we read in D&C 84:109, "Therefore, let every man stand in his own office, and labor in his own calling; and let not the head say unto the feet it hath no need of the feet; for without the feet how shall the body be able to stand?"

How the Scriptures Use the Word *Magnify*

Consider these examples of how the word *magnify* is used in the scriptures. In his epistle to the Romans, Paul wrote, "For I speak to you Gentiles, inasmuch as I am the apostle of the Gentiles, I magnify mine office" (Romans 11:13).

Paul didn't mean that he was expanding his calling (he already *was* the Apostle to the Gentiles). He simply meant that he was fulfilling his responsibilities with exactness and vigor, as confirmed in these scriptures by the prophet Jacob: "And we did magnify our office unto the Lord, taking upon us the responsibility, answering the sins of the people upon our own heads if we did not teach them the word of God with all diligence; wherefore, by laboring with our might their blood might not come upon our garments; otherwise their blood would come upon our garments, and we would not be found spotless at the last day" (Jacob 1:19). And, "Now, my beloved brethren, I, Jacob, according to the responsibility which I am under to God, to magnify mine office with soberness, and that I might rid my garments of your sins, I come up into the temple this day that I might declare unto you the word of God" (Jacob 2:2).

The word *magnify* in this context doesn't mean to multiply, expand, or enlarge. It means to wholeheartedly fulfill, to labor with all of our might.

In Doctrine and Covenants section 88, we read, "Teach ye diligently and my grace shall attend you, that you may be instructed more perfectly in theory, in principle, in doctrine, in the law of the gospel, in all things that pertain unto the kingdom of God, that are expedient for you to understand. . . . That ye may be prepared in all things when I shall send you again to magnify the calling whereunto I have called you, and the mission with which I have commissioned you" (D&C 88:78, 80).

To Magnify Means to Focus and Fulfill Completely

To me, these scriptures indicate not the expanding effect of a magnifying glass, but another of its functions. The magnifying glass can also focus light into precise spots of laser-like energy. These two functions depend on how the magnifying glass is used. If we use the glass to personally observe our stewardship, things look bigger. But if we use the glass to let the light of heaven shine down onto our charges, we create focusing energy instead.

Elder M. Russell Ballard taught, "The instruction to magnify our callings is not a command to embellish and complicate them. To innovate does not necessarily mean to expand; very often it means to simplify" ("O Be Wise," *Ensign*, November 2006). Eliminating or shortening administrative meetings, for example, may be a better way to magnify a calling than adding or lengthening meetings.

Let me give you another example. Another of my favorite responsibilities in the stake presidency is to work with the Primary. One of our stake Primary presidents, Sister Ecklund, decided that she wanted to change the stake training meetings for Primary presidencies. She felt impressed that the training should accomplish more than inspiring leaders to work harder. She wanted instead to provide actual assistance to ward presidencies to help them accomplish their work with the children. So instead of just providing talks about what Primary leaders should or shouldn't do, she and her presidency prepared thick packets of extraordinary sharing time materials for almost every week of every month for every Primary. In the training meetings, they explained the sharing time materials and distributed them, ready to use. They also changed the meeting to be focused on wards instead of stakes. A popular agenda item was when each Primary shared something that was working well or asked for help if there was something that wasn't working well. The meetings were spirit-filled, loving, and practical.

The results of this inspired leadership council magnifying their callings in this way included the sisters in the ward Primary presidencies

Get out of the way of the magnifying glass

feeling that the role of the stake was to lovingly support them—not just supervise or criticize them as secular leaders might. The ward Primary presidencies enjoyed the extra time they had to minister to children because the time-consuming assignment of preparing sharing times had been done for them, and the attendance at stake training meetings for Primary increasing significantly. The sisters knew that they would be receiving high-quality materials and ideas they could use, and they didn't want to miss learning how to use them. These sisters were grateful that their stake Primary leaders, unlike the stake leaders my family member mentioned, magnified their callings.

So How Does a Home Teacher Magnify His Calling?

One of the best answers I ever had to the above question went something like, "Well, I guess that someone who reluctantly went to his families once a month could still report that he had 'done' his home teaching. But I think that when the Lord asks us to magnify our callings that He wants us to really care about the people we home teach, offer them blessings when they are sick, see if they need our help if they are injured or in need, remember their birthdays, keep them in our prayers, and adapt our lessons to the needs of the family."

I think he was right.

How the Lord Magnified His Calling

As our exemplar, the Lord magnified His calling perfectly. What can we learn from His example?

The Atonement was the greatest leadership calling of the Lord. The weight of this responsibility is incomprehensible to us, but it is the only calling we have record of Him displaying any hesitation to fulfill. He didn't question the revelations He received from His Father to organize a church in a hostile environment. He took every opportunity to teach the gospel, often to skeptics and cynics. He confronted the religious and political authorities of His day, lovingly but firmly revealing to them their hypocrisy and iniquity. He cleansed the temple of the leaders of commerce. As His Father willed, He rebuked and cast out evil spirits, made food and drink, healed the sick, cured leprosy, and made the lame walk and the blind see. Through the power of faith, He walked on water, calmed the seas, and changed the weather. He even raised the dead.

Without hesitation, He fulfilled these miraculous aspects of His singular leadership calling as the Lord of the earth, any one of which would cause almost any mortal to shudder with fear and self-doubt, hopeful that the overwhelming responsibility would be lifted or given to another. But only of the culminating responsibility of His redeeming leadership did He pray, "Father, if thou be willing, remove this cup from me: nevertheless not my will, but thine, be done" (Luke 22:42).

In Matthew's account, we also read, "He went away again the second time, and prayed, saying, O my Father, if this cup may not pass away from me, except I drink it, thy will be done. . . . And he left them, and went away again, and prayed the third time, saying the same words" (Matthew 26:42, 44).

We know what happened. The Lord magnified His calling as our Redeemer, despite His understandable concerns. His obedience to the Father and love for all of us overcame His hesitation. His calling couldn't be expanded because it was already the most significant and comprehensive act of leadership in history—the only act to affect the eternal lives of every human who would ever dwell on earth. So He magnified the divine assignment for which He alone was uniquely qualified by doing *exactly* what was required of Him by our Father in Heaven. Nothing more, nothing less. Is there a better example of magnifying a calling than this? Can we do less in our callings and still consider ourselves followers of Christ?

Being Perfect in Christ

I think sometimes we misunderstand the Lord's admonition in Matthew 5:48: "Be ye therefore perfect, even as your Father which is in heaven is perfect" (which is similar to what he told the Nephites in 3 Nephi 12:48, except that He added, "perfect *even as I*, or your Father" [emphasis added]).

Surely He does not mean that He expects us, like Him, to never sin, else why the need for the Atonement? We are all sinners except for Christ (Ecclesiastes 7:20; Alma 34:40). And if we consult the references on the bottom of the LDS scripture page where this admonition is printed, we learn that the Greek word from which this scripture was translated means being "complete, finished, fully developed." Comparing this to the word also translated as "perfect" in a scripture that refers to Noah as a "perfect" man in Genesis 6:9, we learn that the Hebrew word means "complete, whole, having integrity." When the Savior counsels us to be perfect, He is not setting the bar at the unachievable level of complete sinlessness. Instead, He is asking us to have integrity, avoid sin, and become whole through His grace and Atonement.

Similarly, when He asks us to follow His example as a leader and magnify our callings, He is not asking that we complete the same leadership responsibilities He did as the Savior and Redeemer. That would not be possible. Instead, He is asking us to complete our own assignments with the same thoroughness and diligence as He did. That is possible. That is how we can follow Him.

Summary

To magnify a leadership calling doesn't mean to multiply, expand, or inflate it. It means to fulfill it with soberness, vigor, sincerity, and, perhaps most important, honest love for the ones we serve, as our Savior loves us.

In the next chapter, we will discuss how to motivate and inspire those we lead.

CHAPTER EIGHT: HOW TO INSPIRE AND MOTIVATE OTHERS

"But behold, that which is of God inviteth and enticeth to do good continually; wherefore, every thing which inviteth and enticeth to do good, and to love God, and to serve him, is inspired of God" (Moroni 7:13)

W*hen Procter and* Gamble announced that they would be shutting down the Chicago soap plant, Reenie and I began to be receptive to calls from recruiters about other corporate opportunities. We received an attractive dual offer from a company called Tektronix in Portland, Oregon, to work in human resources with significant responsibilities in leadership and team development. The beauty of Portland captured us, so we moved back across the country, closer to our families on the West Coast.

I was called as the Scoutmaster in our new ward and began to see challenges with motivation. Some of the boys worked hard to complete advancements and participate in the outings and activities while others struggled. We had difficulties getting our troop committee staffed and trained for the same reasons. Some of the parents supported the program and others not so much.

People Motivate Themselves

It reminded me of a class Reenie and I had taken on motivation in graduate school. On the first day, the professor welcomed us and proclaimed, "How do you motivate people? The answer is you can't!" I remember thinking, *Great. Why did I sign up for this class?* The professor then said something I have reflected on for years: "The reason that you can't motivate people is that people have to motivate themselves. The best a leader can do is to create an environment in which people feel inspired to do it."

This certainly is consistent with gospel doctrine about agency. A Church leader can't—and shouldn't—*make* anybody do anything. All of God's children have to choose to obey the commandments, not because a leader wants them to, but because that is their personal decision. The right to personal choice is a foundation element of our mortal probation. Brigham Young taught, "Our religion will not permit us to command or force any man or woman to obey the Gospel we have embraced. And we are under no obligation to do this, for every creature has as good a right, according to his organization, to choose for himself" ("The One-Man Power—Unity—Free Agency—Priesthood and Government, Etc.," *Journal of Discourses*, Vol. 14 [London: Latter-day Saints' Book Depot, 1862], 94).

As the Prophet Joseph Smith explained when he answered a query about how he governed those within his stewardship, "I teach them correct principles and they govern themselves" (James R. Clark, *Messages of the First Presidency*, 6 volumes [Salt Lake City: Bookcraft, 1965–75], 3:54).

Glen Tucket, a former baseball coach and athletic director at BYU, explained this important principle when he said, "We're now in an era of motivation. Everything we hear about is motivation this and motivation that. After we conclude a great general conference, people come up to me and say, 'Oh, didn't the speakers at conference motivate you?' I don't mean to be sacrilegious or anything, but my answer to them is, 'No, they didn't motivate me at all, but they surely inspired me to motivate myself'" ("Making Decisions and Feeding Sheep," *New Era*, January 1984).

So how do we as leaders inspire others to motivate themselves? I'd like to suggest four ways: ask good questions, teach pure doctrine, listen to the Spirit, and love them.

Ask Good Questions

I honestly didn't get a lot of traction with my Boy Scouts or the adults who supported them until I applied the method of asking questions to inspire motivation. Instead of trying to be either a cheerleader or an autocrat (promoting or dictating the Scouting program), I saw the most progress when I followed the training I had received by the BSA to make the Scouts a boy-led activity. My role was not to tell them what to do but to ask questions, such as, "What are your personal advancement goals?" Or, "Out of these three camps we looked at, which one looks best to you guys?" Or, "Which skill on this handout I got from the roundtable looks the most interesting to you?"

It was something I had learned back in the factory in Lima. It's hard not to get motivated by your own ideas. The difference between a successful Scout troop and an unsuccessful one is often whether the adult leaders can unleash the discretionary efforts of the boys. Enthusiasm and commitment build as boys plan for what they want to do with their activities and camps. They become motivated.

After working at Tektronix for a few years, I started up a consulting and training company with some colleagues. Eventually, Reenie and I broke off on our own, offering team and leadership effectiveness training to large corporations and government organizations. People tell us that one of the most powerful and practical techniques we teach is a simple idea called Socratic coaching: asking questions to coach or correct instead of just giving advice or prescriptions for action. Instead of saying, "Carl, you need to be more organized in meetings," the leader should say, "Carl, what is your agenda for the next meeting?" Asking the question puts the responsibility squarely on Carl's shoulders, not yours. It gets him to start thinking about solutions, not excuses, and inspires him to motivate himself to act different.

Over the twenty years of teaching this technique, however, we have observed that some types of questions work better than others. Asking open-ended questions—such as, "What is your plan?" for example—is far more effective than asking closed questions, as such questions can be answered with a simple yes or no (such as, "Do you have a plan?").

The reason is obvious. Engaging someone in a conversation allows the leader to discuss, encourage, and develop. A closed question does exactly what it implies. It closes the conversation.

Another type of problematic question is one that implies criticism, such as, "Why did you do that?" Or, "What were you thinking?" Even when the Scouts had made significant mistakes, I found it more useful to ask something like, "What did you learn from that?" I held my tongue when critical thoughts intruded. My patience was usually rewarded. They would talk about their mistakes openly and teach their peers about preparedness, fire safety, or proper food preparation at the same time. Criticism questions, especially when asked publicly, cause people to withdraw, close down, hang their heads, or get angry and defensive.

For example, as a newer stake presidency, we noticed that the ward conference meetings we started having with the bishoprics of each ward weren't as uplifting and Spirit-filled as we had hoped. We took the charge in the CHI seriously where it identified one of the key purposes of a ward conference as to "evaluate activity" and "review the progress of individuals and organizations in the ward" (*Handbook 2: Administering the Church*, 2:18.2.5).

But the leaders sometimes slumped their shoulders and frowned as we reviewed their deficiencies. The mood was not motivational. Little happened as a consequence of the meetings. Even though we were kind and understanding, the ward leaders felt chastised. It was a mistake.

We changed our approach the next year by asking the bishoprics to do something of a self-review of that year's accomplishments. The mood changed as members of the bishopric each spoke about their stewardships and had the opportunity to say what was working and what improvements needed to be made. Interestingly, we often spoke in more detail about problems than before, but when it was the bishopric members themselves who brought up the issues along with their plans to rectify them, they seemed to feel much better about the conversation. And when we showed appreciation for their efforts, asking them questions about their plans—such as, "What do you need to be successful? How can we help you?"—they not only seemed more motivated but were much more likely to take improvement actions than we had seen the previous year. As President Ezra Taft Benson taught,

> In the Church especially, asking produces better results than ordering—better feeling, too. Remember to tell why. Follow up to see how things are going. Show appreciation when people carry out instructions well. Express confidence when it can be done honestly. When something gets fouled up, it is well to check back and find out where you slipped up—and don't be afraid to admit that you did. Remember, our people are voluntary, free-will workers. . . . When you are tempted to reprimand a fellow worker, don't. Try an interesting challenge and a pat on the back instead. (*The Teachings of Ezra Taft Benson*, 376–77)

The Savior Asked Good Questions

As you might suspect, though Socrates was a master of teaching and motivation through questioning, the Savior was *the* master. He had no peer in this regard.

Let's look at some examples. The Lord once asked His disciples, "Whom do men say that I the Son of man am?" (Matthew 16:13). They answered, "Some say that thou art John the Baptist: some, Elias; and others, Jeremias, or one of the prophets" (verse 14). Then the Lord asked the question, "But whom say *ye* that I am?" (verse 15; emphasis added). Peter answered, "Thou art the Christ, the Son of the living God" (verse 16).

A quick read of this incident might suggest that these questions were just an expression of the Lord's casual curiosity. But by asking the questions, Jesus did far more. He gave the disciples the opportunity to develop their own budding testimonies—the motivating power required for gospel action. This was especially important for Peter, who apparently struggled—as we have discussed—with becoming fully converted. The Lord asked these questions to get His disciples to think, evaluate their testimonies, and motivate themselves to be stronger in their commitment to the Lord and building His kingdom.

Church leaders would do well to use this inspired method. What motivates a home teacher to do his home teaching? What motivates a Relief Society president to take time away from her own family to attend a training session? What motivates a Primary teacher to prepare her lesson? What motivates a single parent to get her reluctant kids ready for church? What motivates a less-active brother to return to church and get ready for temple ordinances?

A testimony.

Good questions from leaders help people create or strengthen their testimonies. One of my favorite times as a Scoutmaster was sitting around a campfire after the boys had worn themselves out and stopped poking each other. We listened to animal noises and looked at the stars, and I asked in a moment of silence, "What are you guys feeling right now?" What often followed were some of the best testimonies I've ever heard.

More Questions from the Lord

The Lord used this method of asking questions to inspire motivation many times. In Matthew 20, for example, we read, starting with the verse 30: "And, behold, two blind men sitting by the way side, when they heard that Jesus passed by, cried out, saying, Have mercy on us, O Lord, thou Son of David." Surely the Savior knew why they were calling for Him. Crowds thronged Him at this point of His ministry, asking to be healed. If Matthew, His disciple who wrote the account, could tell that the two men were blind and infer that they wanted to be healed, couldn't the Savior also? But still He asked the question, "What will ye that I shall do unto you?" (verse 32).

He asked a question He already knew the answer to for *their* benefit, not His. Perhaps it was to inspire them to articulate their faith, an essential power in the healing process: "They say unto him, Lord, that our eyes may be opened. So Jesus had compassion on them, and touched their eyes: and immediately their eyes received sight, and they followed him" (verses 33–34).

Many times after performing these miracles, He said, "Thy faith hath made thee whole." (See Matthew 9:22; 15:28; Mark 5:34; 10:52; Luke 8:48; 17:19; and Enos 1:8.) Isn't asking the question of the blind men a way to motivate them to have a similar blessing? Ether taught, "For if there be no faith among the children of men God can do no miracle among them; wherefore, he showed not himself until after their faith" (Ether 12:12).

The Lord repeated this process later with a lame man when He asked, "Wilt thou be made whole?" (John 5:6). Who wouldn't say yes? But in so doing, the Lord again demonstrated how His brothers and sisters can be given the opportunity to play their essential role in the healing process through a declaration of their faith—a declaration motivated by His question.

That the Lord used questions to teach and inspire action is confirmed in the miracle of the feeding of the five thousand. Read this scripture carefully: "When Jesus then lifted up his eyes, and saw a great company come unto him, he saith unto Philip, Whence shall we buy bread, that these may eat? *And this he said to prove him: for he himself knew what he would do*" (John 6:5–6; emphasis added). The purpose of the question was to benefit Philip, not Him. The Lord already knew what He was going to do, but He wanted to provide Philip a way to strengthen his faith by participating in a miracle.

An extraordinary example of this question method is found in Ether 2. The brother of Jared asks the Lord how to light the barges he has built to carry his family across the seas to the promised land. But instead of providing an answer (as He did to the question about air, found in verses 19–21), the Lord asks a question instead. "And he cried again unto the Lord saying: O Lord, behold I have done even as thou hast commanded me; and I have prepared the vessels for my people, and behold there is no light in them. Behold, O Lord, wilt thou suffer that we shall cross this great water in darkness? And the Lord said unto the brother of Jared: What will ye that I should do that ye may have light in your vessels?" (Ether 2:22–23).

And after He explained why windows and fire wouldn't work, the Lord again asked, "Therefore what will ye that I should prepare for you that ye may have light when ye are swallowed up in the depths of the sea?" (Ether 2:25).

Surely the Lord didn't ask these questions because He needed suggestions from the brother of Jared. The Lord knew how to light the vessels, but He wanted the brother of Jared to think for himself and motivate himself to find a way to accomplish the thing the Lord had commanded. As you'll recall, the Lord's question method worked. After some thought, the brother of Jared "did molten out of rock sixteen small stones" (Ether 3:1), which he asked the Lord to touch to provide light during the long journey.

Consider a final example. When the Savior reached out His hand to save Peter from drowning after Peter had tentatively accepted the

Lord's invitation to walk on water, Jesus said, "O thou of little faith, wherefore didst thou doubt?" (Matthew 14:31). What sounds like a chastisement is, I believe, something much more.

If His intention had been to shame Peter, the Lord only needed to say something like, "I'm disappointed in you." But instead, He asked a question. He wanted to inspire Peter to action, to have him become motivated to reflect on the incident, learn something, and do better in the future. Wasn't the Savior inviting Peter to examine and reconcile his doubts so that his faith would eventually be strong enough to perform miracles? Wasn't His question a way to inspire Peter to become as strong as the Lord needed him to be as the next leader of the Church?

When we follow the example of Christ, we do more than preach to our brethren, for example, about the importance of home teaching. We sit down with them, face to face, and ask, "When will you be meeting with the Johnsons again?" Or, "What do you want me to report to the bishop about Sister Gonzales's medical condition?" Thoughtful questions provoke personal evaluation, motivate improvement, and keep responsibility on the person who needs to complete it. We should never ask, "Did you do your home teaching?" Why? At least two reasons: It's a closed question that can be answered with a yes or no that stops the conversation, and home teaching is never done. It's like asking, "Have you completed your assignment as a parent?"

Teach Pure Doctrine

A second principle that helps leaders to inspire members to motivate themselves to higher levels of performance is by teaching pure doctrine. President Henry B. Eyring explained, "We sometimes underestimate the power that pure doctrine has to penetrate the hearts of people" ("We Must Raise Our Sights," *Ensign*, September 2004).

For example, when we read from the scriptures, rehearse the teachings of Christ, or share the words of our prophets, something special happens inside us. People are famished for the want of this doctrine. As it says in Amos, "Behold, the days come, saith the Lord God, that I will send a famine in the land, not a famine of bread, nor a thirst for water, but of hearing the words of the Lord: And they shall wander from sea to sea, and from the north even to the east, they shall run to and fro to seek the word of the Lord, and shall not find it" (Amos 8:11–12).

Teaching doctrine slakes that powerful thirst. And few things inspire like the stories of the valiant who believe in the doctrine and apply it in their lives. Margaret D. Nadauld, when she served as the general president of the Young Women of the Church, said, "I am inspired by the lives of good and faithful women. From the beginning of time the Lord has placed significant trust in them" ("The Joy of Womanhood," *Ensign*, November 2000).

When we teach the Atonement, the plan of salvation, or the power of the priesthood to serve others, wonderful things happen to the motivation level of the listener, who becomes more willing to be a faithful son or daughter of God. This is especially true of what is referred to in the scriptures as the doctrine of Christ: specifically the doctrines of faith, repentance, baptism, the gift of the Holy Ghost, and enduring to the end.

Pure doctrine has a way of piercing the soul and provoking action. I have never seen someone change the way they acted as a home teacher, for example, as a result of hearing that their efforts were reported to the stake presidency or noted in important Church records. Perhaps that would be sufficient in a secular organization, but not in the Church. Something I've seen to be far more effective is the teaching of the doctrine of home teaching—particularly of the importance of loving one another—and having those who have a testimony of home teaching share it with others. Pleading from leaders doesn't work—the Spirit does. That leads to the third way to inspire motivation.

Listen to the Spirit

The Spirit may be the critical resource for inspiring others to motivate themselves to do good works. Here are just three of the many scriptures that teach this principle: "For behold, again I say unto you that if ye will enter in by the way, and receive the Holy Ghost, it will show unto you all things what ye should *do*. Behold, this is the doctrine of Christ" (2 Nephi 32:5–6; emphasis added); "they shall observe the covenants and church articles to *do* them, and these shall be their teachings, as they shall be directed by the Spirit" (D&C

42:13; emphasis added); "and now, verily, verily, I say unto thee, put your trust in that Spirit which leadeth to *do good*—yea, to do justly, to *walk humbly*, to *judge righteously*; and this is my Spirit" (D&C 11:12; emphasis added).

As each of these scriptures indicates, the Spirit clearly has the power to inspire people to motivate themselves to take action. Many refer to this power as "leading." Nephi, for example, explained, "And I was led by the Spirit, not knowing beforehand the things which I should do" (1 Nephi 4:6). And of the Savior, we read, "Then was Jesus led up of the Spirit into the wilderness to be tempted of the devil" (Matthew 4:1).

Mark's account of this incident is even stronger. It says, "And immediately the Spirit *driveth* him into the wilderness" (Mark 1:12; emphasis added). We should not conclude from these last two examples that either Nephi or the Lord lost their agency on these occasions, of course. They could have chosen not to follow the powerful lead of the Spirit, but they didn't; they chose to follow. We should choose to follow the Spirit too.

Using the Spirit

Because the Spirit is such an essential part of effective Church leadership, I will discuss it in much more detail in several subsequent chapters. But as it relates to motivation, let me suggest a few ways to use the Spirit during our leadership interactions.

First, opportunities to motivate others can occur at any time. A wise leader will therefore live worthily so that he or she can be directed by the Spirit whenever necessary. If a leader runs into neighbors at the store, or sees them in the street, a leader who is sensitive to the promptings of the Spirit has a better chance of saying the right words to inspire others to motivate themselves than a leader who isn't being directed. Sometimes those conversations occur at the times you'd least expect them—when, for example, a distraught friend calls to discuss a problem, or a child asks a question in the car on the way to school. This requires vigilance in maintaining personal worthiness so that we can recognize and respond to promptings. I have often found myself offering a silent prayer when one of these situations occurs. And I always try to pray to be directed by the Spirit when preparing a talk, activity, lesson, or meeting.

Second, when the Spirit prompts us as leaders to do or say something, we must do it. If we say the words that we are directed to speak, the Spirit will confirm their truthfulness and increase the probability that the person or persons we are working with will feel inspired.

Third, do the things in our homes and meetings that are conducive to the Spirit. Don't forget to open and close meetings with prayer. Sing the hymns of Zion. Remember that spiritual music is a type of prayer: "yea, the song of the righteous is a prayer unto me" (D&C 25:12). Avoid contention and other things that diminish or repel the Spirit. The wrong type of music, for example, can quickly drive the Spirit away.

Fourth, use the scriptures. Instead of summarizing or paraphrasing, open the scriptures and read from them directly. There is a special spirit that comes from reading or speaking the actual canonized word of God. Given the option of either talking about or quoting from the scriptures, the inspiring leader will follow the example of Christ and use the verbatim words of God, even if it takes a few extra moments to remember or locate them. I've been in training sessions with General Authorities several times when they ended the meeting with a question and answer session. I am always in awe when they answer a question by quoting or reading the scriptures. I have seen it many times and have always felt the Spirit when their knowledge and use of the scriptures blessed and inspired me to motivate myself to do better. This is what the Lord did.

Love Them

The final way to help people motivate themselves is to love them. This is also the way the Savior did it. Love was such a core element of the Lord's ministry that, like His Father, it defined Him, as John the Beloved explained, "And we have known and believed the love that God hath to us. *God is love*; and he that dwelleth in love dwelleth in God, and God in him" (1 John 4:16; emphasis added). A few verses later, "We love him, because he first loved us" (1 John 4:19).

It is difficult to think of something the Savior did that wasn't motivated by love. He was a perfect exemplar of what He referred to as the two greatest commandments: "And one of the scribes came, and . . . asked him, Which is the first commandment of all? And Jesus answered him, The first of all the commandments is . . . thou shalt love the Lord thy God with all thy heart, and with all thy soul, and with all thy mind, and with all thy strength: this is the first commandment. And the second is like, namely this, Thou shalt love thy neighbour as thyself. There is none other commandment greater than these" (Mark 12:28–31).

His love of the Father motivated the Lord to obey the commandments, pray, worship, study, teach the gospel, cleanse the temple, and fulfill his divine responsibilities. "If ye keep my commandments, ye shall abide in my love; even as I have kept my Father's commandments, and abide in his love" (John 15:10).

And from the everlasting flow of love He has for all of us, he motivated Himself to heal the sick, raise the dead, and offer up His life as an atoning sacrifice. As John wrote, "Greater love hath no man than this, that a man lay down his life for his friends" (John 15:13).

How does this apply to the Christlike leader? Perhaps the greatest learning about how the Savior loved His fellow men was that His love was nonselective. He healed the ungrateful lepers as well as the grateful one. He healed the severed ear of the soldier who had come to the Garden of Gethsemane to capture Him, just as He healed the dead loved one of His dear friends.

Can we do the same? Does the president of the Young Women save her love for the young women who are most lovable, or does she demonstrate equal love for those who roll their eyes or peer at the floor and answer her in monosyllables? Does a counselor in the Young Men presidency love the star athlete and the clumsy or rebellious boy alike? Does the Relief Society president love both the families who express gratitude for the meals they received as well as the ones whose only communication is to express displeasure for the menu? Does the elders quorum president feel the same about the boisterous man whose boys gave his son a black eye as he does the brother who is trying so hard to attend church and be a good home teacher?

As President N. Eldon Tanner taught, "To be an effective leader or teacher one must show love and actually feel love for the person he is trying to instruct. No power is as motivating as the power of love. Christ loved everyone—the weak, the sinner, and the righteous. Sometimes the ones who need to be loved most are the ones who seem to deserve it the least" ("Leading As the Savior Led," Liahona, January 1978). President

Ezra Taft Benson added, "A love of people is essential to effective leadership. Do you love those whom you work with? Do you realize the worth of souls is great in the sight of God (see D&C 18:10)? Do you have faith in youth? Do you find yourself praising their virtues, commending them for their accomplishments? Or do you have a critical attitude toward them because of their mistakes?" (*The Teachings of Ezra Taft Benson*, 370).

Charity Never Faileth

The Savior's love is so powerful that we give it a special name: charity, the pure love of Christ. Though this attribute is normally associated with His shepherding competency, as mentioned in an earlier chapter, it serves as the foundation for all of His leadership, including His roles as an exemplar, scholar, believer, seeker, disciple, and teacher.

Without charity, why would He have healed the physically, emotionally, and spiritually ill? How could He have patiently taught those who despised Him? How could He have withstood the abuse heaped upon Him? How could He have motivated Himself to ask the Father to forgive those who hung Him on the cross?

Can we follow His example of loving the unlovable? Of loving those who don't look, act, or think like we do? Can we love our enemies as He asked us to do?

He loves us, and He explained that if we love Him, we will motivate ourselves to keep the commandments (John 14:15). Perhaps He commanded us to "love one another, as I have loved you" (John 13:34; 15:12) partly because He knew that this is the most effective motivating force that we could share with each other. What power on earth can motivate like the pure unconditional love of a mother, husband, or sibling? Elder Gene R. Cook wrote, "Love is a divine motivation; it motivates the Lord and thus must also motivate us. Particularly is that so in dealing with our families" (*Raising Up a Family to the Lord* [Salt Lake City: Deseret Book, 1993], 176). President Henry B. Eyring also taught, "Love is the motivating principle by which the Lord leads us along the way toward becoming like Him, our perfect example" ("Our Perfect Example," *Ensign*, November 2009).

The leaders of His day criticized the Lord for loving others. Despite His explanation that the sick, not the well, were the ones who needed a physician, hypocrites protested that His association with sinners was a way of condoning their sins. How smug they must have felt to know that they would never lower themselves to associate with unworthy brothers and sisters. The Lord, of course, felt no such constraint. Thankfully.

If we want to follow the Savior, perhaps we too should patiently sit with someone who has made some bad choices without judging him or her at all, just in the way that we hope that the Savior will sit with us one day.

Hate the Sin, but Love the Sinner

Ultimately, only He who was sinless could demonstrate perfectly through His associations that you could hate sin without hating the sinner. Moreover, it was His love for the imperfect—meaning everyone on earth other than Him—that usually motivated people to repent. Who isn't touched by His interaction with the adulteress? After saving her life by suggesting to those who had assembled to stone her that whoever was without sin should cast the first stone, He refused to condemn her, saying, "Woman, where are those thine accusers? hath no man condemned thee? She said, No man, Lord. And Jesus said unto her, Neither do I condemn thee: go, and sin no more" (John 8:10–11).

He lovingly responded to the pleas of the blind, lame, and leprous for merciful healing. He lovingly responded to the families of Lazarus and the daughter of Jairus, who pled that their dead might be raised again to life. He lovingly forgave those who betrayed and crucified Him. Even those He had to chasten, He did so with love. Peter, he who thrice denied knowing Him, the Lord lovingly made the next leader of His Church.

Perhaps we can learn to love like this too. Maybe we can look at others who have made mistakes for their potentials instead of their pasts. Maybe we can forgive those who hurt us and leave the responsibility of judgment to the Lord.

Love Casteth Out Fear

Why was His love such a powerful motivating force? Part of the answer is found in 1 John 4:18: "There is no fear in love; but perfect love casteth out fear: because fear hath torment. He that feareth is not made perfect in love."

When we feel loved, the fear of recrimination and failure decreases. Love drives out these and other fears as well: the fear of rejection, isolation, manipulation, uselessness, loneliness, shame and so on. Love breeds hope, optimism, and faith. It makes us feel that it is possible for us to repent and be more like our Savior, especially the pure type of love described in 1 Peter: "Seeing ye have purified your souls in obeying the truth through the Spirit unto unfeigned love of the brethren, see that ye love one another with a pure heart fervently" (1 Peter 1:22).

Unfeigned love is the motivating force used by the Savior, not guilt. A Christlike leader never tries to motivate others with guilt. As Elder M. Russell Ballard cautioned, "I hope it goes without saying that guilt is not a proper motivational technique for leaders and teachers of the gospel of Jesus Christ. We must always motivate through love and sincere appreciation, not by creating guilt" ("O Be Wise," *Ensign*, November 2006).

Summary

Technically, a leader is unable to motivate anyone to do anything. But the Christlike leader—who asks good questions, teaches pure doctrine, listens to the Spirit, and genuinely loves others—can inspire those within his or her stewardship to motivate themselves to live the gospel fully.

In the next chapter, we will review why we both minister and administer in the Church.

CHAPTER NINE: WHY WE NEED TO BOTH MINISTER AND ADMINISTER

"Verily, verily, I say unto you, this is my gospel; and ye know the things that ye must do in my church; for the works which ye have seen me do that shall ye also do; for that which ye have seen me do even that shall ye do" (3 Nephi 27:21)

*A*fter Reenie and I started up our own consulting and training firm, we often received requests from our clients that went something like this: "Please come in and teach our supervisors how to be leaders instead of managers." The popular thinking of the time was that the tasks of leadership—things like being a visionary and an effective agent of change—were more important than the more mundane role of management, including things like planning, organizing, and budgeting. And while there is some truth to the idea that leadership is more critical to the success of an organization than management, our clients inevitably discovered that their leaders needed to be skilled at both.

Ministering versus Administering

We face a similar dichotomy in the Church. A helpful way to distinguish the types of tasks we face as leaders is to divide them into two columns, as illustrated in Figure 9-1. In one column, we list those activities associated with ministering, including things such as teaching, blessing, providing ordinances and assistance, and visiting the sick and the needy. In the other column, we list activities associated with administering the Church, including meeting to plan and coordinate our efforts, scheduling our facilities, and accounting for and distributing the sacred funds of the Church. Obviously, the ministry must be prioritized above what we'll call the "administry."

To conduct endless ward council meetings, for example, that never result in action to bless the lives of others is a shameful waste of time and energy. As Elder M. Russell Ballard said, "The primary purpose of Church leadership meetings should be to discuss how to minister to people. Most routine information and coordination can now be handled through phone calls, e-mails, or regular mail so that agendas for council meetings and presidency meetings can focus on needs of the people" ("O Be Wise," *Ensign*, November 2006).

But it is important to remember that both the ministry and the administry are essential. What good does it do, for example, to go to the homes of the sick and needy, only to find that a lack of an appointment prohibits the visit? Can we distribute welfare funds to those who need it if fast offerings are never collected—or worse, if fraudulent use or poor accounting practices have depleted the resource for those who truly need it? Can we enjoy the blessings of a temple if we don't have the administrative processes in place to plan, fund, and build one?

Figure 9-1: Selected Differences between Ministering and Administering

	Ministering	**Administering**
Illustrative tasks	Teaching, testifying, blessing, ordaining, leading, baptizing, confirming, sealing, forgiving, visiting, praying, counseling, comforting, healing, inspiring, and so on	Organizing, planning, scheduling, financing, recording, preparing, budgeting, indexing, managing, standardizing, auditing, constructing, cataloging, reporting, and so on

Typical callings	Visiting teacher, home teacher, gospel doctrine teacher, gospel essentials teacher, auxiliary teacher, seminary or institute teacher, temple ordinance worker, proselyting missionary, patriarch, Apostle, prophet, and so on	Visiting teacher coordinator, executive secretaries, clerks, Scout committee members, high councilors, stake specialists, temple laundry worker, mission office missionary, stake auditors, and so on
Sample activities	Visiting widows, less-active, and ill members; teaching Spirit-filled lessons and conducting meaningful testimony meetings at girls' camp; making the Church more effective; providing welfare assistance for the needy; speaking at general conference; and providing temple ordinances	Organizing visit appointments and schedules; arranging for camp meals, staffing, and transportation; making the Church more efficient; collecting and accounting for fast offerings; arranging for conference broadcasts; and building temples

The current subtitle of the CHI is *Administering the Church*—evidence that we as leaders need to do well in both columns. The reason, in fact, that you'll notice callings like Relief Society president, auxiliary heads, and bishop are not included in either column is that they have a fairly even mix of both ministering and administering responsibilities. (That is likely true of our modern-day prophets, seers, and revelators as well, but I've listed them in the ministering column because that is the part of their role that is most apparent to the rest of us).

Once again, we have only to look at the example of the Savior to see that both ministering and administering responsibilities are necessary for Church leaders.

The Lord's Ministry

Most of the information we have about the Lord's life focuses on His ministry. And because this is the key function of His leadership we will delve into this in much more detail in later chapters on His extraordinary teaching and shepherding competencies.

For the purposes of this chapter, however, let's quickly review a wonderful summary of the Lord's ministry found in a simple verse penned by Matthew: "And Jesus went about all Galilee, teaching in their synagogues, and preaching the gospel of the kingdom, and healing all manner of sickness and all manner of disease among the people" (Matthew 4:23).

He taught, preached, and healed *all manner* of sickness and disease—physical, emotional, mental, and spiritual. And he did all this by being among the people. Why did He do that? We know that He performed His ministry to obey His Father, but, as John indicated, there were other reasons as well: "Now before the feast of the passover, when Jesus knew that his hour was come that he should depart out of this world unto the Father, having loved his own which were in the world, he loved them unto the end" (John 13:1).

We know that many believed in His teaching and miracles and that they followed him (see John 2:23). As the number of His followers grew, it eventually became necessary to create an administry to support His ministry.

The Lord's Administry

One of the first things the Lord did to establish an administry was to organize His Church, as we have discussed in earlier chapters. He called Apostles, a Quorum of Seventy, and others to create a formal structure, with distinct relationships and responsibilities. This allowed organized institutional support for teaching the gospel in perpetuity and for *administering* the saving ordinances through proper priesthood authority. As Latter-day Saints, we believe that the Lord's original Church was restored by Joseph Smith in modern times, as noted in Articles of Faith 1:6: "We believe in the same organization that existed in the Primitive Church, namely, apostles, prophets, pastors, teachers, evangelists, and so forth."

Other elements of the administry include standardization of doctrine and prescribed patterns for important religious practices. The Savior taught, for example, about the importance of properly teaching what He referred to as the doctrine of Christ: "There shall be no disputations among you, as there have hitherto been; neither shall there be disputations among you concerning the points of my doctrine, as there have hitherto been. . . . And this is my doctrine, and it is the doctrine which the Father hath given unto me" (3 Nephi 11:28, 32).

There are also many well-established patterns in the administry for devotional acts, such as proper prayers. For example, about personal prayer, the Lord taught, "After this manner therefore pray ye: Our Father which art in heaven, Hallowed be thy name. Thy kingdom come. Thy will be done in earth, as it is in heaven. Give us this day our daily bread. And forgive us our debts, as we forgive our debtors. And lead us not into temptation, but deliver us from evil: For thine is the kingdom, and the power, and the glory, for ever. Amen" (Matthew 6:9–13). Notice that in this instance, the Lord did not require a word-for-word recitation, as in all ordinance prayers. But He did teach the proper pattern of prayer. He, of course, offered many prayers that are recorded in the scriptures, each following the general pattern of addressing the Father, expressing gratitude, and asking for blessings. These prayers are beautiful, genuine, and appropriate to the task at hand.

Administering Ordinances

The administration of ordinances requires special diligence. Of baptism, for example, Christ taught,

> Baptism is to be administered in the following manner unto all those who repent—the person who is called of God and has authority from Jesus Christ to baptize, shall go down into the water with the person who has presented himself or herself for baptism, and shall say, calling him or her by name: Having been commissioned of Jesus Christ, I baptize you in the name of the Father, and of the Son, and of the Holy Ghost. Amen. Then shall he immerse him or her in the water, and come forth again out of the water. (D&C 20:72–74)

In this same section, the sacrament prayers are also revealed. These prayers, along with the baptism prayer, are to be repeated word for word: "It is expedient that the church meet together often to partake of bread and wine in the remembrance of the Lord Jesus; And the elder or priest shall administer it; and after this manner shall he administer it—he shall kneel with the church and call upon the Father in solemn prayer" (D&C 20:75). Verses 77–79 then reveal the exact wording of the prayers. Missing even a word of this sacred ordinance requires correction.

The Savior was the first one to administer the sacrament: "And as they did eat, Jesus took bread, and blessed, and brake it, and gave to them, and said, Take, eat: this is my body. And he took the cup, and when he had given thanks, he gave it to them: and they all drank of it. And he said unto them, This is my blood of the new testament, which is shed for many" (Mark 14:22–24).

We still administer the sacrament as He did and use the prescribed prayers to provide consistency across all wards in the Church. Similarly, of the proper administration of the sealing ordinance in the temple, the Savior taught,

And again, verily I say unto you, if a man marry a wife, and make a covenant with her for time and for all eternity, if that covenant is not by me or by my word, which is my law, and is not sealed by the Holy Spirit of promise, through him whom I have anointed and appointed unto this power, then it is not valid neither of force when they are out of the world, because they are not joined by me, saith the Lord, neither by my word; when they are out of the world it cannot be received there . . . *for my house is a house of order*, saith the Lord God. (D&C 132:18; emphasis added)

Other Administrative Responsibilities for Leaders

There are other elements of the administry that are also prescribed because the Lord's house is "a house of order." For example, there are minimum ages for baptism and certain priesthood ordinances. There are worthiness standards for some advancements and entering the temple. Certain priesthood authority is required for particular ordinances. Some reports need to be completed and funds managed and accounted for. Similar meeting schedules and ward organizations are used across the world. A wise, Christlike leader becomes familiar with these and other administrative requirements found in the CHI so that his or her appointed stewardship is administered properly. As the Lord said, "It is wisdom in me; therefore, a commandment I give unto you, that ye shall organize yourselves and appoint every man his stewardship; That every man may give an account unto me of the stewardship which is appointed unto him. For it is expedient that I, the Lord, should make every man accountable, as a steward over earthly blessings, which I have made and prepared for my creatures" (D&C 104:11–13).

Spiritual Gifts for the Administry

Fortunately, as in any important aspects of Church leadership, we can have divine assistance to complete this portion of our callings. For example, there are spiritual gifts available to help with the administry. In Doctrine and Covenants, we read, "For all have not every gift given unto them; for there are many gifts, and to every man is given a gift by the Spirit of God. To some is given one, and to some is given another, that all may be profited thereby" (D&C 46:11–12).

In addition to many wonderful gifts listed in this section that assist with the ministry (faith, healing, miracles, prophecy, tongues, and so on), we read of gifts pertaining to the administry as well:

> And again, to some it is given by the Holy Ghost to know the differences of administration . . . it is given by the Holy Ghost to some to know the diversities of operations . . . to some is given, by the Spirit of God, the word of wisdom. To another is given the word of knowledge, that all may be taught to be wise and to have knowledge. . . . And unto the bishop of the church, and unto such as God shall appoint and ordain to watch over the church and to be elders unto the church, are to have it given unto them to discern all those gifts lest there shall be any among you professing and yet be not of God. (D&C 46:15, 17–18, 27).

Remember Revelation

The CHI has other information about the administry, some of which is subject to adaptation through revelation. But in his concluding remarks of the Worldwide Leadership Training Meeting in November

2010, Elder Boyd K. Packer warned, "As the Church has grown in size, it always seems to grow in complexity. There are so many programs and procedures that need to pull together in harmony. We all wish for patterns of administration that mirror the simplicity of the gospel" ("Concluding Remarks," *Worldwide Leadership Training Meeting*, November 2010).

He goes on to quote from President J. Reuben Clark Jr., speaking for the First Presidency, who said, "The work of the Church, in all fields, is standing in grave danger of being regimented down to the minutest detail. The result of that will be that not only will all initiative be crushed out but that all opportunity for the working of the spirit will be eliminated. The Church has not been built on that principle" (Ibid., quoting from "Memorandum of Suggestions," March 29, 1940, 4).

This powerful warning helps us remember that while the administry is necessary, it should never negatively affect the more important ministry of the Church.

Examples of the Importance of Proper Administry

Why is the administry necessary? In my experience, it is because improper administry can cause unnecessary conflict and offense. A bishop who doesn't have consistent administrative procedures in place to schedule buildings, for example, may create hurt feelings when one family is allowed to use the building and another is not. A stake without procedures that govern child of record baptisms may find inconsistent practices take root in different wards, potentially leading to jealousy or confusion. Inconsistent application of the CHI could result in the evolution of doctrinal impurity. When offended over administrative incompetence, families who leave the Church can plunge multiple future generations into bitterness and inactivity.

A certain amount of administry is even necessary in positions I've listed in Figure 9-1 as being primarily ministerial callings. A Sunday School teacher, for example, may do a wonderful job creating spiritually significant lessons, but if he or she consistently runs overtime, the youth he or she teaches may lose an opportunity to participate in important priesthood or Young Women classes. Or, if the doctrine he or she teaches is incorrect, he or she may confuse or misdirect students. A faithful visiting teacher, who may excel in the ministerial part of her calling in terms of providing comfort and solace, may unintentionally offend or even harm her well-loved responsibilities because she prefers not to pay attention to less important administrative details of her assignment, such as scheduling appointments or tracking food allergies.

Summary

The key work of a Church leader is related to the ministry, following the pattern exemplified by the Lord. But effective leadership also requires administrative competencies. The Christlike leader understands this and strives to be effective in both ministering and administering the work of the Lord. He or she pays special attention to the most important aspects of the adminstry, such as the proper functioning of the Church, the teaching of correct doctrine, and the accurate administration of ordinances.

One administrative task that most leaders will need to do especially well if the work is to progress properly is facilitating effective meetings, the subject of the next chapter.

Chapter Ten: How to Lead Meetings

"The elders are to conduct the meetings as they are led by the
Holy Ghost, according to the commandments and revelations
of God" (D&C 20:45)

*I*n our professional capacity as leadership trainers, Reenie and
I often hear complaints about meetings. Some say, "They drag on
way too long." Or, "We don't accomplish anything." Many see
them as a distraction from the real work.

Common Meeting Problems and Opportunities

We've heard similar concerns from Church members about administrative meetings, such as presidency, training, council, and committee meetings, specifically:

- "I'd much rather be with my family than spend time planning to do something that will probably never happen."
- "Ward council meetings where everybody reports on their auxiliary activities instead of talking about the needs of ward members seem like a waste of time to me."
- "Why do we have to go to a special meeting when this could have been covered in our regular meetings?"
- "We spend too much time hearing from the leader. Why doesn't he [or she] ask for our ideas?"

- "We could have accomplished everything in this meeting with a email or phone call. It wasn't necessary to take us away from our families for this."

Conversely, we've also heard

- "I'm excited about the plan we put together to help the Sanchez family next Thursday night."
- "I loved that family history training. My daughter and I went straight home, got on the computer, and found a family name to take to the temple."
- "I loved it when the group leader said that he felt impressed to end the meeting and take us all over to Sister Landry's apartment. When she answered the door, she had tears in her eyes. She told us she had been praying someone would visit."
- "I liked how the youth led the meeting instead of the adults. It gave me goosebumps."

What is the difference between a good meeting and a bad one? And what does a leader have to do to make them as effective as possible?

Worship Meetings

We learn in the scriptures that it is incredibly important to honor the Sabbath day and keep it holy. Our Sunday meetings help us do that and renew our covenants through the partaking of the sacrament. Sabbath meetings allow us to teach, learn, edify, and strengthen one another. As noted in Mosiah: "And there was one day in every week that was set apart that they should gather themselves together to teach the people, and to worship the Lord their God, and also, as often as it was in their power, to assemble themselves together" (Mosiah 18:25).

Because only a few of our ward and stake leaders are directly involved in leading worship meetings, however, this chapter will focus primarily on how to effectively lead administrative meetings.

Administrative Meetings

For those of us who serve in leadership callings, there are many more meetings to attend and lead than our worship services. The Lord acknowledges that these administrative meetings are important: "And now, behold, I give unto you a commandment, that when ye are assembled together ye shall instruct and edify each other, that ye may know how to act and direct my church, how to act upon the points of my law and commandments, which I have given" (D&C 43:8).

Though we have extensive scriptural guidance about Sabbath day worship services (sacrament, Sunday School, priesthood, Relief Society, Young Men's, Young Women's, Primary, and so on), there are fewer examples from the life of the Savior about how to lead administrative meetings—but the ones we have are instructive.

For example, in D&C 6:32, the Lord said, "Verily, verily, I say unto you, as I said unto my disciples, where two or three are gathered together in my name, as touching one thing, behold, there will I be in the midst of them—even so am I in the midst of you."

Five Tools for More Effective Meetings

I believe we can assume at least three things about leading administrative meetings effectively. First, the Lord knows that administrative meetings are necessary ("The several elders composing this church of Christ are to meet . . . to do whatever church business is necessary to be done at the time" [D&C 20:61–62]). Second, we can expect (assuming that unworthiness doesn't prohibit it) that His presence can guide us during those meetings. Third, our meetings need to have a clear, meaningful, and commonly understood purpose ("touching one thing" [D&C 6:32]).

In our training practice, we suggest that there are many things that are important for good meetings, including preparation, the right participants attending, good facilitation of the meeting by the leader to keep things moving, starting and stopping on time, and so forth. But perhaps the five most important tools for effective administrative Church meetings are using an agenda, creating a practice of returning and reporting, using good information, intervening to balance the "administry" with the ministry, and—most important—ensuring our meetings are guided by the Spirit, as if the Lord Himself were in our midst.

Tool 1: Using Agendas

Let's review these five key meeting tools one at a time. In the CHI, we read, "Leaders prepare an agenda for each meeting or assign someone else to prepare it under their direction. An agenda helps participants focus on the meeting's purposes and use time effectively. It should be prioritized to ensure that the most important matters are discussed first" (*Handbook 2: Administering the Church*, 2:18.1).

See Figure 10-1 for an example of an agenda for an administrative meeting. This particular agenda is from one of my stake presidency meetings I selected at random. While I have attempted to preserve as much of the actual agenda as possible (to show you an authentic example), names of people outside of the presidency and certain references have been deleted to ensure confidentiality.

Figure 10-1: Sample Stake Presidency Meeting Agenda

Stake Presidency Meeting	Cedar Mill Oregon Stake Stake Presidency Meeting—Agenda October 25, XXXX
Participants Stake presidency Stake clerk Stake executive Secretary (*Book 2*, Section 18.3.5)	Opening Prayer: President Fisher Leadership Training: None Next—President Fisher
Principles In councils, leaders meet under the direction of presiding officers to discuss ways to help individuals and families. Guided by the Holy Ghost, they work together to determine effective ways to serve members of their organizations (*Book 2*, Section 3.2.2).	**President Bair:** 1. Give Bill access to new patriarchal system. 2. Approve the form for submission of the new bishop (today). 3. Send the three hymns to President Goodfellow for stake conference. **President Goodfellow:** 1. Stake conference music. 2. Complete music for annual HP meeting. 3. Contact Sister XXXX regarding location of records. **President Fisher:** 1. Seek XXXX's assistance for indexing and ordinance goals. 2. Take another look into the operation of the DI pod. 3. Get information out to wards to advertise the annual HP quorum meeting.

Effective councils invite full expression from council members and unify their efforts in responding to individual, family, and organizational needs (*Book 2*, Section 4.1). Agenda may include:
• Counsel together about stake matters.
• Plan ways to strengthen individuals and families.
• Evaluate wards, high priests groups, elders quorums, activities, and auxiliaries.
• Create plans to implement instructions from scriptures, Church leaders, and handbooks.
• Identify members to call to Church positions.
• Review the bishops' recommendations of members to serve missions and of brethren to be ordained elders or high priests.
• Report on assignments, plan meetings, review stake calendar, and review the stake budget.

Karl Taylor:
1. Make appointments for President Bair to meeting presidencies as well as the HC for fifteen minutes each.
Bill Ensign:
1. Contact XXXX about XXXX's issue.

Out of Town
President Bair: December 30–January 3
President Goodfellow: November 9–13
President Fisher: November 23–December 8
Bill Ensign: October 26–28, November 30–December 22
Karl Taylor: November 24–28

Missionaries Returning
• Elder XXXX (SK), Finland, Helsinki November 12 (PDX, Thursday, 8:20 p.m.)

Missionaries Needing to Be Set Apart
• Sister XXXX (SP), New York, Utica, October 28
• Sister XXXX, Japan, Tokyo, November 4
• Elder XXXX (FO), South Africa, Durban December 3

Topics for Next PEC Meetings
• Expectations of high councilors and their assignments—next meeting
• CM stake vision
• Callings/releases—principles
• HC responsibility for ward rescue work participation in quorum meetings
• Upcoming calendar items (next thirty days)
• October 30, presidency social
• November 8, meeting with bishoprics
• November 12, stake temple day
• November 21–22, stake conference

Next Meeting	**Priesthood Advancements and Ordinations**
November 1 (1 hour) 6 a.m.	• XXXX (SP), advance to elder—waiting for paperwork
Opening Prayer: President Goodfellow	• XXXX (SH), advance to high priest— waiting for interview
Training: None	
Closing Prayer: President Fisher	**Staffing**
	• Stake Primary secretary
XXXX Ward	**Bishop's Interviews**
Meeting Times	Missionary Work, 80 percent goal for HT,
FO 9-12	Sabbath day observance, sacrament meeting
TA 11-2	talks, fast offerings, stake activities, staffing
BE 1-4	forms, timing of callings, online contributions
OH 9-12	
SK 11-2	**Individual Member Needs**
SH 1-4	XXXX, XXXX
WV 9-12	
RC 11-2	Reporting on duties and responsibilities high
SP 1-4	councilors (monthly during two hour, SPM)
	• November 8—President Fisher

Discussion Items
• Stake conference planning (speakers/prayers)
• PPIs for high councilors
• 'My Plan' for returning missionaries
• Stake council agenda items

Presidency Specific Items
• President Bair:
• President Goodfellow:
• President Fisher:
• Bill Ensign:
• Karl Taylor: Stake RS presidency steward-
  ship interview schedule?

Closing Prayer: Karl Taylor
Upcoming beyond thirty days—

Clear Purpose

Note a few things from this sample agenda that I felt, as a meeting participant, were especially helpful to us.

First, you'll see in the left-hand column that we've listed the purpose of this particular meeting, as stated in the CHI. This is helpful for prioritizing the items on our agenda, which we seldom are able to complete within the time allotted. I can think of several examples of where someone in the meeting reviewed that column and asked a question that would have moved us past an item that was less critical and onto one more clearly consistent with our meeting purpose. The power of posting this information on the agenda is that the entire burden of keeping the meeting prioritized to accomplish our purpose is not exclusively on the shoulders of our stake president.

Second, there are a number of items on this agenda that help us be more efficient. The assignments at the top of the page, for example, remind us at the beginning of each meeting to report out on the assignments that our stake president gave us the week before. The lists of missionaries to be called and released, details of travel schedules, and upcoming calendar events facilitates our planning and scheduling but consumes only minutes of our meeting, allowing us to spend more time focusing on strengthening individuals and families (usually through discussions listed here as topics for PEC meetings, priesthood advancements, bishop's interviews, and individual member needs).

Third, there are a number of items on the agenda that help us feel the Spirit in the meeting. For example, we always open and close the meeting with prayer. This allows us to pray for guidance, confirm staffing recommendations, and ask for blessings for those in need. We have specifically been advised to incorporate prayer into these meetings by the Savior: "And behold, ye shall meet together oft . . . ye shall pray for them unto the Father, in my name. Therefore, hold up your light that it may shine unto the world. Behold I am the light which ye shall hold up—that which ye have seen me do. Behold ye see that I have prayed unto the Father, and ye all have witnessed" (3 Nephi 18:22–24).

Each meeting also has special training assigned beforehand from the scriptures, CHI, Worldwide Leadership Training, *Preach My Gospel*, and *Come Follow Me* curriculum (or other resources as assigned by our stake president).

Fourth, the way we use the agenda offers lots of opportunities for us to increase our effectiveness in the meeting. Karl, our stake executive secretary, sends out the agenda at least three days ahead so it can be modified with new issues and concerns. That makes the agenda more current and captures a lot of the "surprises" that otherwise have to come up during the meeting itself without sufficient time for prayerful preparation prior to discussion. During the meeting itself, the leader might also bring up the agenda to ensure that the meeting is moving according to plan by saying something like, "We are taking a little longer on this item than we planned. Should we continue discussing it and drop something else off the agenda, or should we continue this discussion in our next meeting and move to the next item on the agenda?"

Alternative Approaches

This certainly isn't the only way to do an agenda. The important thing is to find something that works for you. I have a friend named Lewis Hassell who served as a counselor to then Bishop Mitt Romney (prior to Governor Romney's nomination to be the Republican candidate for the president in 2012). Lewis often spoke of how Bishop Romney ran bishopric meetings, especially how he always put people in need as the first item on every agenda—a lesson Lewis later put into practice as a bishop and stake president.

Other Methods for Prioritizing Agenda Topics

The idea that agendas should be prioritized is a good one. I have already discussed how the CHI meeting purpose statement has helped us. I've seen other organizations use their goals to the same effect.

The Lord offered another suggestion: "Then one of them, which was a lawyer, asked him a question, tempting him, and saying, Master, which is the great commandment in the law? Jesus said unto him, Thou shalt love the Lord thy God with all thy heart, and with all thy soul, and with all thy mind. This is the first and great commandment. And the second is like unto it, Thou shalt love thy neighbour as thyself. On these two commandments hang all the law and the prophets" (Matthew 22:35–40).

You might look at your agenda and ask, "Which of these items affect the two greatest commandments?" and move the ones that do up toward the first of the meeting and the ones that don't to the bottom of the agenda. This leads to the second tool of effective Church meeting management.

Tool 2: Creating a Practice of Returning and Reporting

The "return and report" feature in the agenda example above is the list of names with assignments. Each week, we are accountable to the other members of the presidency to publicly report the status of our assignments. This keeps us accountable and ensures that our meeting discussions result in actions that affect those we serve. The pattern of return and report is well established in the gospel and is an essential part of administrative meetings.

Those who have been to the temple will recognize this pattern demonstrated between the Father and the Son. As always, the Lord is our finest example of accepting assignments, completing them, and then reporting on their satisfactory completion.

In an *Ensign* interview with President Dieter F. Uchtdorf and Elder M. Russell Ballard, the Apostles taught, "That's what we learn in the temple—the return-and-report principle. But some of our leaders are somehow afraid to give direction, to provide a kind but clear message of what is expected, and then to follow up" ("Tending the Flock: Teaching Leadership Skills to Youth," *Liahona*, June 2008). President Marion G. Romney also confirmed, "Remember, brethren, to return and report is the final act of the faithful and wise steward" ("Welfare Services: The Savior's Program," *Ensign*, October 1980). Sister Ruth Funk, then general president of the Young Women, added,

> When a young person is called to serve, the responsibilities that go with the call are outlined. With this stewardship comes the responsibility to give an accounting. That is, we receive direction, we carry out our responsibility, or we "do it" as President Kimball says, and then we return and report what we have done and receive further counsel and direction. This accounting is scheduled at regular intervals with a member of the bishopric but should also be a daily accounting with the Lord who will bless and magnify those whom he calls to be his leaders. (" 'Exceeding Young,' " *Ensign*, June 1977).

As another rule of thumb, an effective Church leader *only* gives assignments that he or she plans to follow up on using the return-and-report principle modeled by the Savior. If the assignment doesn't warrant follow-up, it probably isn't important enough to be issued at all. Follow-up is one of the most important things to do in a meeting. But the way we do it is important. President Ezra Taft Benson instructed, "When responsibility has been given, the leader does not forget the person assigned nor his assignment. He follows with interest but does not 'look over the shoulder.' He gives specific praise when it is deserved. He gives helpful encouragement when needed. When he feels that the job is not being done and a change is needed, he acts with courage and firmness but with kindness. When the tenure of an office has been completed, he gives recognition and thanks" (*God, Family, Country: Our Three Great Loyalties* [Salt Lake City: Deseret Book, 1974], 140).

Tool 3: Using Good Information

The third tool for effective meeting management is using good information. If the meeting requires making decisions, solving problems, planning, discussing, or any of the many meeting processes required to make something happen in your area of stewardship, then good information is essential. Though leaders are often tempted to take action based on conjecture, assumptions, partial or potentially inaccurate information to save time and effort, this approach almost always ends up becoming problematic. I know, for example, of families who went for extended periods of time without Church contact because of outdated information about their former desire to not have home or visiting teachers assigned. Feelings have been hurt when an auxiliary leader responded to one account of a problem between two youth without getting the other side of the story as well. Incorrect information can cause ward leaders to under- or over-serve the needy in their wards, misallocate roles, make poor decisions, or fail to solve problems effectively.

I recall a lecture in one of my graduate school classes when the professor asked the question, "How do you know how someone feels about something?" Expecting him to reveal some marvelous diagnostic tool or share some amazing insight about how leaders can intuit the true feelings of others, we remained silent. "There is only reliable method," he continued. "You have to ask them."

Good information gathering requires work. If you want to know how the youth feel about one activity versus another, ask them. If you want to know if the sisters will support a course of action, ask them. If you are trying to figure out why a home teacher isn't visiting his families, ask him. You might be surprised with answers. And the better the quality of information you use to inform your decisions, the better the quality of the decisions.

Tool 4: Intervening to Balance the Administry with the Ministry

Let's move to the fourth tool of effective meeting management. The CHI states, "Leadership meetings should focus on strengthening individuals and families. Time spent on calendaring, program planning, and other administrative business should be minimal" (*Handbook 2: Administering the Church*, 18.1).

Though meeting leadership roles have both ministerial and administrative components, a common leadership error is losing the appropriate balance between them. It's especially problematic for the administry to strip away time and effort from the ministry. This is certainly not the way the Lord led. If we learn nothing else from the paucity of stories about His divine techniques for administration, we should learn that the ministerial work has to be the first priority. Said another way, the sole purpose for the administry is to enable the ministry.

How does a leader ensure this? One important way is to drive all meeting discussions toward action. As Paul taught in his epistle to the Hebrews: "And let us consider one another to provoke unto love and to good works: Not forsaking the assembling of ourselves together, as the manner of some is; but exhorting one another: and so much the more, as ye see the day approaching" (Hebrews 10:24–25).

Talking about people's problems without developing a plan to assist them is not the Lord's way. The leader might ask, "What can we do to help the Ma family?" Or, "How could we get the Ramos children to Primary?" Or, "Who can visit Brother Sato in the hospital?" When administrative meetings don't lead to action, meetings lose their reason for existing.

I love the stories about how President Ezra Taft Benson used to facilitate meetings. He worked hard to convert discussion into action, and after "he felt that adequate discussion had taken place, he typically said, 'I think we've got enough hay down now. Let's bale a little,' bringing the issue to resolution" (Sheri L. Dew, *Ezra Taft Benson: A Biography* [Salt Lake City: Deseret Book, 1987], 429).

A leader will also try to balance the time in meetings so that the ministry is prioritized. Sometimes he or she may need to intervene and redirect conversations back to rescue work, preparations for ordinations, gospel instruction, missionary work, or other essential elements of the gospel. As a rule, if some good ministerial work does not result from a meeting, then that meeting was a waste of time.

Tool 5: Ensuring Our Meetings Are Guided by the Spirit

The fifth and most important tool for effective Church meeting management is to ensure that the Spirit guides our meetings. The Lord repeated this admonition in many ways. While instructing the Twelve on their new roles and responsibilities, for example, He said, "But when they deliver you up, take no thought how or what ye shall speak: for it shall be given you in that same hour what ye shall speak. For it is not ye that speak, but the Spirit of your Father which speaketh in you" (Matthew 10:19–20). And to modern-day elders (also including the Apostles in this case), He reiterated through the Prophet Joseph that "the elders are to conduct the meetings as they are led by the Holy Ghost, according to the commandments and revelations of God" (D&C 20:45).

We see this pattern anciently in the Book of Mormon: "And their meetings were conducted by the church after the manner of the workings of the Spirit, and by the power of the Holy Ghost; for as the power of the Holy Ghost led them whether to preach, or to exhort, or to pray, or to supplicate, or to sing, even so it was done" (Moroni 6:9). And, of course, it was also the pattern established after the Holy Ghost was given to the Lord's Apostles in the Old World: "And when they had prayed, the place was shaken where they were assembled together; and they were all filled with the Holy Ghost, and they spake the word of God with boldness" (Acts 4:31).

These scriptures pertain to both worship and administrative meetings. And the Spirit is certainly no less important in administrative meetings than those for the whole Church population. For example, if decisions are not confirmed by the Spirit—and if agenda items are not planned, executed, or modified by it—then the meeting is nothing more than a secular meeting. It may be elegant administratively, but it will probably accomplish little for the ministry.

Summary

The good news is that the Lord has provided a method for administering the Church. The bad news is that this method is called meetings. But this is only bad news if leaders don't lead meetings effectively. When Church leaders use agendas, the divine pattern of returning and reporting, good information, prioritize the ministry over the administry, and ensure that meetings are guided by the Spirit, Church administrative meetings can be more productive and uplifting than their secular counterparts.

An essential competency of effective meeting leadership is working with councils—the topic of the next chapter.

CHAPTER ELEVEN: HOW TO WORK
IN AND WITH COUNCILS

"Verily, thus saith the Lord, the time is now come, that it shall be disposed of by a council, composed of the First Presidency of my Church, and of the bishop and his council, and by my high council; and by mine own voice unto them, saith the Lord" (D&C 120:1)

*A*fter working for some wonderful corporations in a variety of management and staff assignments, Reenie and I eventually started our own consulting company. We decided to help organizations develop stronger leaders and teams, using ideas from our graduate studies, organizational experiences, and written works. We were blessed with success as we traveled the globe to help some of the most powerful corporations and government agencies in the world. It came as no surprise to us that some of our best work was inspired by our Church leadership experiences, especially those related to the use of councils.

The first Church leadership meeting recorded in the scriptures occurred in the premortal existence. It was a council, often referred to as the Grand Council in Heaven. Our ward and stake councils, as well as our presidencies, bishoprics, and family councils, are examples of contemporary organizations based on this long-established form of governance used since the time preceding the creation of the earth. As Elder M. Russell Ballard explained, "It has never been God's intention that His children stand alone in important decisions and responsibilities.

During our premortal existence, He Himself called for a grand council to present His glorious plan for our eternal welfare. His Church is organized with councils at every level, beginning with the Council of the First Presidency and the Quorum of the Twelve Apostles and extending right on through to our stake, ward, and family councils" (*Counseling with Our Councils: Learning to Minister Together in the Church and in the Family* [Salt Lake City: Deseret Book, 1997], 11).

Unique Characteristics of Councils

As you probably know, councils operate differently than other organizations. Elder Ballard illustrated the difference by relating a story of how he conducted training on the proper functioning of councils throughout the Church. He felt dismayed when he asked several bishops to roleplay how a ward council might develop a plan to activate a fictional less-active family.

Unfortunately, the bishop would always identify a solution to the problem and make assignments without discussing the matter with the council first. Inevitably, Elder Ballard had to stop the training and ask the bishop to repeat the exercise, asking for ideas and recommendations—especially from the sisters—*before* making any decisions (see *Counseling with Our Councils: Learning to Minister Together in the Church and in the Family*, 4). I strongly recommend Elder Ballard's book for your leadership library. It is inspired. The chapter on disciplinary councils is especially helpful to anyone who is blessed with the opportunity to participate in the application of the Atonement to those within their ward or stake stewardship.

The doctrinal support of the council concept is scriptural. In Doctrine and Covenants, for example, the Lord revealed the fundamental leadership structure of the Church: "And this shall be your business and mission in all your lives, to preside in *council*, and set in order all the affairs of this church and kingdom" (D&C 90:16; emphasis added).

Working in a Council When You Aren't the Leader

Scriptural advice isn't limited to leaders of councils. John Whitmer, for example, was specifically instructed to participate more in these types of leadership meetings: "Again, verily I say unto you that he can also lift up his voice in meetings, whenever it shall be expedient" (D&C 47:2).

Everyone is a member of a council where they are not the leader. And just as the leader has a role, the participant does as well. Speak up. Make suggestions. Share your inspiration with others. When President Russell M. Nelson was a newly called member of the Quorum of the Twelve Apostles, he was initially reluctant to share his opinion. "But [President Benson] wouldn't have that," he reported. "In fact, if I was silent on something he would draw it out" (Sheri L. Dew, *Ezra Taft Benson: A Biography*, 430).

Participatory Nature of Councils

Councils are highly participatory. Their strength comes from the collective wisdom and experience of many instead of only one. But unlike some of the "team concept" facilities I worked in during my consulting career, the council is not a democratic organization where the majority opinion wins the day. The concept of leadership authority, keys, and revelation is still essential in the Lord's Church (as we have previously discussed). Nevertheless, an effective council is far more likely to help an auxiliary, ward, or stake reach its full potential in important areas (such as missionary work, temple work, and rescue work) than a leader working in isolation.

For example, a council that discusses a problem together will generate more ideas to work with. They are also more likely to implement solutions they create than ones assigned by leaders. They may have access to more information and be uniquely qualified through friendships and experiences to effectively approach a wider variety of people and situations. As President Ezra Taft Benson instructed, "No wise leader believes that all good ideas originate with himself. He invites suggestions from those he leads. He lets them feel that they are an important part of decision making. He lets them feel that they are carrying out their policies, not just his" (*The Teachings of Ezra Taft Benson*, 371).

In the 2010 Worldwide Leadership Training Meeting, a ward council meeting was demonstrated. Following the demonstration, selected members of the Quorum of the Twelve Apostles, General Presidency of the Relief Society, and First Quorum of the Seventy commented about what they saw.

Elder David A. Bednar observed, "I think we have the mistaken notion that every element of revelation coming to the ward has to come through the bishop. By virtue of his keys, he has to acknowledge it and affirm it, but he doesn't necessarily have to be the only vehicle through whom it comes." Sister Julie B. Beck added, "I think that the ability to counsel in the Lord's way is really counterculture in every culture in the world. It's difficult in families and homes. It's difficult for everybody" (M. Russell Ballard, with Jeffrey R. Holland, David A. Bednar, Walter F. Gonzalez, and Julie B. Beck, "Panel Discussion," *Worldwide Leadership Training Meeting*, November 2010).

As noted by the scripture that opened this chapter, leadership councils are the method required by the Lord to govern His Church. Surely the one time when councils would have seemed unnecessary for Church governance was when the Lord Himself led the ancient Church. Why put leadership groups in place when the Master could simply make divine decisions Himself and assign followers to execute His perfect and holy will? But He didn't do that. He organized leadership councils when He called the Quorum of the Twelve and the First Quorum of the Seventy. There are a multitude of reasons for doing this, not the least of which was likely to develop future Church leaders.

So how can we make our councils more effective?

Eight Tips for Making Councils More Effective

In addition to the tips shared in the previous chapter on facilitating effective meetings, councils can either benefit or be derailed by a few especially important leadership practices.

Tip 1: Facilitate, Don't Dominate

Councils blossom under facilitative leaders who ask questions and invite discussion instead of issuing assignments. Though there are times when a leader is prompted by the Spirit to take a specific course of action, these promptings will normally occur after a robust discussion of the issues at hand, following the pattern established in Doctrine and Covenants 9, which suggests a certain level of preparation before revelation can be expected. A leader that dominates council discussions or influences the outcomes prematurely reduces both the quantity and quality of ideas as humble council members acquiesce to the leader they have agreed to sustain.

For example, rather than say, "Sister Walker, I think it would be a good idea for you to visit the Cannons and invite them to return to church," you might say, "I'm concerned about the Cannons. Does anyone have any ideas about how we could get them back to church?" In the discussion that follows, it might become clear that someone other than Sister Walker is better suited to extend the invitation, or that an entirely different approach—such as recommending that Sister Cannon be called to serve as her daughter's activity day leader—is more appropriate.

I cannot tell you how many times as a bishop I felt the Spirit confirm someone else's idea as we were discussing it—an idea that likely never would have surfaced if I had made an assignment prior to the discussion. As a rule of thumb to avoid dominating councils as a leader, consider this suggestion: share the problem, not the solution. Sharing problems opens communication. Sharing solutions closes it.

Tip 2: Encourage Participation

Though some members are eager to participate in leadership councils, others require encouragement. An elders quorum president, for example, during a presidency council meeting might have to invite his shy second counselor to participate by asking something like, "Juan, what do you think we should do about our disappointing home teaching results from last month?"

We can also encourage participation by asking for council members to share proposals. A bishop who feels impressed to find a way to help children in the ward avoid the problems, for example, of early introduction to pornography might ask a Primary president to have her presidency pray about a solution and be prepared to share a proposal with the ward council in the following meeting.

This is apparently the method used in the Grand Council in Heaven. We read in Abraham, "And he [God] stood in the midst of them. . . . And the Lord said: Whom shall I send? And one answered like unto the Son of Man: Here am I, send me. And another answered and said: Here am I, send me. And the Lord said: I will send the first. And the second was angry, and kept not his first estate; and, at that day, many followed after him" (Abraham 3:23, 27–28).

From this account, we learn several things about how our Father facilitated this council: several attended and participated actively, the leader didn't dominate, a proposal was shared with the council (see the Lord's plan in verses 24–26), and the leader asked a question to invite participation before making His decision.

In an attempt to create participation, however, avoid falling into the round-robin trap. A round-robin council meeting is one where all participants are assigned to do status reports for every meeting. These routine report meetings can quickly devolve into mind-numbing sessions that leave insufficient time for prioritized future planning and problem-solving. They leave participants always looking in the rearview mirror instead of out of the windshield at the road ahead. You will crash.

Tip 3: Don't Micromanage

Sometimes in our anxiety to produce results, we claw back decision-making and problem-solving responsibilities from council members. This is often called micromanagement, and it is highly demotivating, even if it is unintentional on the part of the leader. If a counselor in a presidency, for example, is given an assignment to lead an activity and the leader then swoops in and takes it over, the counselor feels disempowered. The counselor is unlikely to feel good about accepting responsibilities in the future, worried that his or her efforts may be hijacked or undermined by the leader.

The same feeling comes when leaders make decisions that should rightly be made by others. Ironically, though the leader steps in and takes these actions to improve results, it will often do the opposite. The rightful decision maker will normally disengage, forcing the leader to continue assuming his or her responsibilities. We will speak of this thorny problem in more detail in the later chapter on delegation.

Elder M. Russell Ballard discussed other reasons why micromanagement is problematic. Cautioning that it's not uncommon for adult leaders to hijack responsibility that actually belongs to the youth, he advised, "Instead, a leader should bring the matter into a council setting with the members of the quorum presidency and ask, 'What are we going to do, how are we going to do it, and who's going to do what?' If youth see a bishop or another leader who runs everything, who doesn't involve others, and who doesn't bring into council all the resources that he has, the youngsters are going to think that's what a leader does" ("Tending the Flock: Teaching Leadership Skills to Youth").

Tip 4: Summarize and Clarify

A valuable role that a leader can play in a council meeting is to summarize and clarify council discussions and decisions. Though an effective meeting facilitator shouldn't dominate a meeting, he or she should help to keep it on track and on time. A good way to do this is to periodically summarize discussions by saying things such as, "We've heard some wonderful ideas about how to help our new investigators. It sounds like our best approach might be to ask the Smiths to be the fellowshippers for Mark and Amy, and see if we could get one of the Laurels to invite their daughter Savannah to the skating activity on Friday. Is that right?" A summary like this allows council members to support or disagree and drives the discussion to an appropriate conclusion.

Tip 5: Make Assignments as Directed by the Spirit

Having a discussion is only the first part of an effective council meeting. At some point, the leader must ensure that some action is planned as a result. Listen to the Spirit to determine the most appropriate approach. You might say something like, "We've agreed that we should invite the Sanchez family to the fireside next Sunday evening. Maria could you do that this week and report back at our next meeting?" Or ask for a volunteer by saying, "Who would like to extend the invitation to the Sanchez family?"

Remember the pattern for a quick planning activity suggested by Elder Ballard above. Ask, What are we going to do? How are we going to do it? Who's going to do what? (I'd also suggest adding timeframes.) When will it be done?

Finalized assignments should be recorded. One way to do this is to keep brief meeting notes that are distributed to all participants after the council meeting.

Tip 6: Follow Up

As already mentioned in the previous chapter on meeting management, it is better to not make an assignment than to make one that won't be followed up on. Understandably, leaders are often eager to address more current needs and sometimes overlook previous commitments. But once things are selectively followed up on, council members quickly learn that it isn't necessary to feel accountable for accomplishing assignments. This is a common but damaging leadership mistake.

Create a workable method to follow up on all assignments. For example, in the sample stake presidency agenda shown earlier in the book, you saw a list of assignments at the beginning of each agenda so that a return-and-report practice could be established that follows the pattern demonstrated in the temple for how our Savior and Heavenly Father act as council leaders.

Tip 7: Support Council Members

Leaders can sometimes unintentionally undermine those whom they have a stewardship over. This is often a result of wanting to help members who come to them directly with disagreements with someone reporting to the leader. Though there may be times when a bishop, for example, has to reverse a decision made by a Sunday School presidency, a leader of the Young Men has to change the direction of a teachers quorum president, or a president of the Young Women has to override an adviser, these reversals should be rare, because they can create self-doubt, disempowerment, and discouragement in the person who has been corrected.

When possible, it is far better to support the other members of your leadership council and urge those with concerns to try a little harder to resolve their issues directly with the proper authority (instead of you). If a change needs to be made, work with that council member directly and encourage them to be the one that makes the revision rather than having it come from you. Don't undermine their authority or allow them not to learn from a mistake by taking things over from them yourself. Consider this advice from President Ezra Taft Benson, who served as both a senior Church and senior government leader: "A good leader . . . does not overrule unless he first confers with him whose decision he overrules. He does not embarrass an associate before others" (*The Teachings of Ezra Taft Benson*, 371).

One of my professors, Stephen Covey, shared a personal experience about how important it is to support those you lead. He served as a mission president in Ireland while still in his thirties and was concerned about his first meeting with his area supervisor. During the meeting, some of the branch and district presidencies who were also in attendance voiced concerns directly to the area supervisor about issues that were part of the new mission president's stewardship. Instead of addressing the issues himself, the supervisor said, " 'These, of course, are for your mission president's attention. I'm here to sustain and help him. He will deal with these matters' " ("How Do You Get Others to Be Self-Motivated?" *Ensign*, February 1972).

The Church leaders would have continued to look to the senior leader for guidance—had the authority started to solve the problems himself—instead of to the mission president. Brother Covey reported that he felt sustained by his leader: "How responsible I felt! How committed! How motivated to make things work! How open I was to his teachings of correct principles and help" (Ibid.).

This approach is smart for another reason as well. Once a senior leader begins to assume the responsibilities of other leaders, he or she will have to continue shouldering the work that should be done by others. It is not a sustainable leadership strategy.

Tip 8: Praise Accomplishments

Sometimes in our anxiety to hasten the work of the Lord, we forget to take the time to praise council members for a job well done. This is inconsistent with the actions of a Christlike leader. Just as we all strive someday to hear from the Lord, "Well done, thou good and faithful servant" (Matthew 25:21), so should we acknowledge the effective service offerings of council members. Your acknowledgements needn't be grand or flowery, and they should avoid becoming the "praise of men" discouraged by the scriptures.

Usually, an authentic thank you will do, but another way to praise the work of council members is to help them understand the consequences of their work by discussing the baptisms, rescues, advancements, or temple ordinances that have resulted from their efforts. The Spirit will touch them, and they will know that their work is meaningful and has helped a son or daughter of God. President Benson taught, "Even harder to bear than criticism, oftentimes, is no word from our leader on the work to which we have been assigned. Little comments or notes, which are sincere and specific, are great boosters along the way" (*The Teachings of Ezra Taft Benson*, 371).

This acknowledgment is helpful during the councils as well. In the Worldwide Training Meeting previously mentioned, Elder Walter F. Gonzalez said, "For me it was wonderful that [the bishop] also—and some of the counselors as well—praised [the council members'] comments. That's important in every culture. It's always good to praise contributions and good ideas of others. That brings unity and also builds Zion, of course, and promotes revelation and inspiration. People feel more comfortable to share their best ideas, and it opens the door for more . . . of the Spirit" (M. Russell Ballard, with Jeffrey R. Holland, David A. Bednar, Walter F. Gonzalez, and Julie B. Beck, "Panel Discussion," *Worldwide Leadership Training Meeting*, November 2010).

A Note on Family Councils

Perhaps the most important council on Earth is the family council. Arguably, we wouldn't even be here if they didn't exist. What would have happened if Adam and Eve had skipped the family council where Eve convinced Adam to reprioritize his thinking about the relative importance of the commandments? Absent that council, Adam may still have remained in the Garden of Eden alone, with all of humankind languishing in a premortal state of existence.

It is a wise family that learns how to adapt the council concept to their unique situation (considering the ages and abilities of children) so that members can learn how to exercise their agency, strengthen their testimonies, and accept their responsibilities within the safety of the home environment. Councils are how our Heavenly Father leads His family. Is it difficult to imagine that He expects less of us than to follow His divine example for the governance of our own families here on earth?

Summary

Eight tips for leading councils include the following: facilitate, don't dominate; encourage participation; don't micromanage; summarize and clarify; make assignments as directed by the Spirit; follow up; support council members; and praise accomplishments.

In the next chapter, we will discuss a related topic—delegation.

CHAPTER TWELVE: HOW TO DELEGATE

"Thou wilt surely wear away, both thou, and this people that is with thee: for this thing is too heavy for thee; thou art not able to perform it thyself alone" (Exodus 18:18)

We moved back to Portland after a few years away in Federal Way, Washington. I was called to serve on my second high council. Though I preferred teaching callings in the ward to administrative ones in the stake, I knew it was what the Lord required of me, and so I did it. I came to enjoy serving closely with a wonderful stake presidency and eleven other faithful men. I looked forward to my weekly assignments.

One evening, about four years into my calling, the stake president telephoned me. "Brother Fisher," he said. "We are considering names for a new bishop in your ward. I wanted to get some recommendations from you."

Four odd things happened in rapid succession. First, my mind went totally blank. I didn't feel good about recommending anyone. It was the most blatant example I had ever experienced of a stupor of thought. Second, I had an incredible feeling of love for everyone in our ward wash over me. Third, I had an impression that I would be called as the bishop. And fourth, the names of three brethren came into my mind—a first counselor, a second counselor, and a counselor to be called at a later date to replace one of my original counselors.

I said nothing about this, of course, to my stake president. Instead, I asked him for a little time to think about recommendations. He agreed. A day or so later, I emailed him five names for possible bishops, which was a simple task for a ward that had as much significant leadership talent in it as ours did.

I did, however, mention my impressions later on to my wife. She was incredulous because of my brutal travel schedule. At that time in my consulting career, I spent 60 to 70 percent of my time traveling out of town.

About a month later, our stake president invited my wife and me to meet with him at the stake center. He called me to serve as bishop. He asked me how much time I needed to think about counselors. I told him I didn't need any. We reviewed my impressions, and he said that these experiences were not unusual with bishops.

But I know of several who were not forewarned as I was. I have come to believe that some of us need a little more time to prepare ourselves. Others are just ready. We once had the pleasure of having then-Elder Dieter F. Uchtdorf of the Twelve as a visiting authority at a stake conference.

He spoke in the priesthood leadership meeting of how he had been surprised by each of his leadership callings. Having seen his leadership capability for several years now, *I'm not surprised* that he had no advance notice from the Lord. I don't think he needed it. He also noted that in his experience reorganizing stakes, he sometimes met several worthy men in a single stake who told him that each of them had received an impression that they were to be called as the new stake president. He confessed to being bothered by this, until he felt inspired that the Lord sometimes gave people these experiences about a potential calling when He considered them capable and worthy of being called—whether they would actually receive that calling.

My personal learning from his talk was that these impressions are tender mercies that should not be shared outside of our own families unless the calling is made. They certainly shouldn't be expressed in an attempt to influence someone charged with extending the calling. As mentioned in previous chapters, the authorized revelation about who should be called (not just who is qualified, capable, or worthy) goes to the keyholder or to the one to whom the keyholder has delegated the assignment.

I had served as bishop's counselor before and thought I knew something about what it meant to be a bishop. I was wrong. It was far more time-consuming and difficult than I thought it would be. I still remember my first bishops welfare council meeting, where all the bishops in the stake met together. They were kind enough to each offer a little advice. One of them looked at me sternly and said, "Delegate or die."

Delegate or Die

He wasn't the first to offer that advice. When Moses was bending under the load of his calling, his father-in-law Jethro told him a similar thing:

> And it came to pass on the morrow, that Moses sat to judge the people: and the people stood by Moses from the morning unto the evening. And when Moses' father in law saw all that he did to the people, he said, What is this thing that thou doest to the people? why sittest thou thyself alone, and all the people stand by thee from morning unto even? . . . The thing that thou doest is not good. Thou wilt surely wear away, both thou, and this people that is with thee: for this thing is too heavy for thee; thou art not able to perform it thyself alone. Hearken now unto my voice, I will give thee counsel, and God shall be with thee: . . . thou shalt provide out of all the people able men . . . and it shall be, that every great matter they shall bring unto thee, but every small matter they shall judge: so shall it be easier for thyself, and they shall bear the burden with thee. (Exodus 18:13–22)

Sounds like Jethro's version of "delegate or die."

Finding Balance

Without delegation, few Church leaders could be successful, and some might even harm their families. Elder M. Russell Ballard observed, "Occasionally we find some who become so energetic in their Church service that their lives become unbalanced. . . . They refuse to delegate or to allow others to grow in their respective responsibilities. As a result of their focusing too much time and energy on their Church service, eternal family relationships can deteriorate. Employment performance can suffer. This is not healthy, spiritually or otherwise" ("O Be Wise," *Ensign*, November 2006).

Similarly, King Benjamin counseled, "And see that all these things are done in wisdom and order; for it is not requisite that a man should run faster than he has strength" (Mosiah 4:27).

Preparing Future Leaders

Delegation is important not only to share the workload of the ministry but also to prepare future leaders as well. When President Spencer W. Kimball spoke on the topic of leadership to the Young Presidents organization, he explained why the Savior led in this manner: "Other leaders have sought to be so omnicompetent that they have tried to do everything themselves, which produces little growth in others. Jesus trusts His followers enough to share His work with them so that they can grow. That is one of the greatest lessons of His leadership" ("Jesus: The Perfect Leader," from an address delivered to the Young Presidents organization, Sun Valley, Idaho, January 15, 1977).

But delegation is not as simple as turning over work to others. That's why many leaders don't do it. It requires planning and coaching, often taking more time in the beginning than if the leader simply does the job by himself or herself. "Delegation is not just a gimmick to get rid of work. It is a leadership strategy—a larger plan in which the leader is eventually relieved of certain activities and the person receiving tasks experiences growth and development in the new area of work. Effective delegation is the result of serious planning, a clear explanation of what is involved, proper training, follow-through, and a willingness to let go" (William G. Dyer, "Why, How, and How Not to Delegate: Some Hints for Home and Church," *Ensign*, August 1979).

Brother Dyer instructed that leaders can delegate assignments (a single task), projects (a more complex set of tasks), or areas of work (a complex set of activities that persists over time). Depending on what is delegated, the leader must invest increasingly significant amounts of time, energy, and trust. And Brother Dyer warned, "Any good leader knows, however, that delegation won't necessarily give him more free time immediately. In the long run, effective delegation should give the leader more time for other matters, but in the short time frame, it may involve an even greater time commitment" (Ibid.).

How the Lord Delegated

Let's consider six of the Savior's delegation practices in more detail by looking primarily at how He delegated responsibilities to Peter, the senior Apostle of the Church.

1: Use Proper Church Structure and Authority

As previously mentioned, the Lord established a church that relies on delegated authority. There are only a few keyholders, and these key-holders delegate the authority to work within stewardships appropriate to the scope of the keyholder. Even the Lord's authority was delegated by the Father, as noted by President Ezra Taft Benson: "Many times Jesus reminded people that His mission on earth was one through delegated authority. . . . In speaking to the Jews in the synagogue, Jesus told them that He had been delegated [to] by His Father: 'For I came down from heaven, not to do mine own will, but the will of him that sent me' (John 6:38)" (*The Teachings of Ezra Taft Benson*, 378).

The Lord set the pattern for the inspired structure of the Church by calling Apostles and the Quorum of the Seventy, whom He commissioned to carry on the work in His name. At the Mount of Transfiguration, heavenly messengers bestowed the keys to the First Presidency of the Church—Peter, James, and John—and all those who receive the keys thereafter can trace them back to this glorious event. As President Benson again observed, "Jesus gives us the master example of good administration through proper delegating. . . . He called twelve Apostles to assist Him in administering the Church. He also called the Seventy. He delegated [to] others. There were to be no spectators in His Church. All were to be involved in helping build the kingdom. And as they built the kingdom, they built themselves" (Ibid.).

The Lord instructed that all delegated authority to Church leaders comes directly from Him: "Therefore, whatsoever ye shall do, ye shall do it in my name; therefore ye shall call the church in my name; and ye shall call upon the Father in my name that he will bless the church for my sake" (3 Nephi 27:7).

2: Give Significant Responsibility, Not Just Minor Tasks

When the Savior delegated, He gave significant responsibility and was neither paternalistic nor condescending. He instructed Peter, for example, to "strengthen his brethren"—an assignment with broad scope and significance (Luke 22:32). To the Twelve, He gave the assignment to "go ye into all the world, and preach the gospel to every creature" (Mark 16:15), and He delegated power over unclean spirits and the responsibility to heal all manner of sickness and disease (Matthew 10:1).

Peter took his assignments seriously. At the day of Pentecost, three thousand souls were "pricked in their heart" and accepted his invitation to "Repent, and be baptized . . . in the name of Jesus Christ" (Acts 2:37–38). Five thousand more believed his message a few days later in Jerusalem (Acts 3:19; 4:4).

This delegated authority culminated in Peter raising a beloved woman from the dead in the way he had observed the Savior raise a child: "But Peter put them all forth, and kneeled down, and prayed; and turning him to the body said, Tabitha, arise. And she opened her eyes: and when she saw Peter, she sat up. And he gave her his hand, and lifted her up, and when he had called the saints and widows, presented her alive" (Acts 9:40).

When he healed a lame man, Peter made clear from whence this delegated authority had come, saying, "Why look ye so earnestly on us, as though by our own power or holiness we had made this man to walk? . . . Jesus, whom ye delivered up . . . his name hath made this man strong" (Acts 3:12–16).

Note that the Lord didn't restrict the autonomy or agency of others by requiring a particular methodology for accomplishing the responsibilities he delegated. Instead, He expected others to figure out their own best method of accomplishing the assignment He gave them.

3: Be Clear about the Responsibility and Its Importance

The Savior was clear in delegating responsibility and helping people understand the importance of the delegated task. At the sea of Tiberias, for example, He instructed Peter to "feed my lambs" (John 21:15). To add emphasis and ensure understanding, He repeated the instruction twice more, using the slightly different words: "feed my sheep" (John 21:16–17).

Interestingly, before delegating out this responsibility, the Savior reminded Peter of why the assignment was so important—and why

Peter must motivate himself to accomplish it—by preceding the delegation with the question: "Lovest thou me?" Thus, motivated by the love of his Savior, the same Peter, who in his weakness, had thrice denied the Christ eventually became a leader so powerful in his delegated authority that people would line the streets "that at least the shadow of Peter passing by might overshadow some of them" and heal them (Acts 5:15).

Though Christ was the cornerstone, Peter would become *Cephas*— a stone, or, in the words of Elder Jeffrey R. Holland, "a principal building block for the priestly foundation" of the Church ("The Lengthening Shadow of Peter," *Ensign*, September 1975).

Surely the Lord knew that His efforts to teach, develop, and delegate to Peter would be worth it in the end. Can we have less faith in those we are charged to develop, even when they seem unable to accomplish the tasks required?

4: Show Confidence That the Person Can Accomplish the Responsibility

When the Lord instructed Peter to launch out into the deep and cast his net over the side of his boat, Peter had been laboring mightily all night and was certain that there were no fish to be caught. Nevertheless, something about the Lord's confident instruction caused him to cast in his net one more time. And the size of the catch threatened to burst the net and capsize two vessels. But a much bigger test of faith and obedience was yet to come.

As Peter reached the shore of Galilee, the Lord invited him to leave his profession and accept a delegated assignment as a disciple of Jesus Christ and future leader in the Church. This faithful, humble man, inspired by the confidence the Lord showed in him, abandoned everything—not just his livelihood, but everything he knew and trusted, his associations, his community, his life. The scriptures say simply of this life-rocking event that Peter "forsook all, and followed him" (Luke 5:11). Can you imagine what it would take to forsake *everything*?

Though this says much about Peter, it also says something about the way the Lord delegated. Even with assignments that seemed life-shattering, massive, incomprehensible, or impossible, when the Lord delegated some authority or assignment, He did it in a way that made people think they could accomplish what He expected of them. Can you imagine being in a boat in stormy seas and watching the Savior approaching you, walking on the water? Can you imagine Him extending His hand to you and inviting you to join Him on the rocking sea? But when He delegated the power to master the elements to Peter, He did it in a way that inspired the brave man to jump overboard, where he briefly "walked on the water, to go to Jesus" (Matthew 14:29).

Nephi understood this when he declared, "I will go and do the things which the Lord hath commanded, for I know that the Lord giveth no commandments unto the children of men, save he shall prepare a way for them that they may accomplish the thing which he commandeth them" (1 Nephi 3:7).

A modern-day leader would certainly not ask something of a follower that would shatter his or her faith, esteem, or abilities. We have to assume that the Lord asked extraordinary things of Peter because He knew that this great leader, with faith and effort, could walk on water, heal the sick, and raise the dead. But to a new or struggling member, an assignment to do missionary work or speak at church may seem just as impossible to them as walking on water did to Peter. They need to develop their confidence in delegated assignments and authority that are appropriate to them, just as Peter did in those assignments that were appropriate to him. This confidence will be a byproduct of the Spirit's confirmation, which should drive any discussion of delegated responsibility.

But it should also be derived from the feeling that the leader will help the person to whom he or she has delegated responsibilities to accomplish their assignment. The delegatee should feel that the leader would always be available to answer questions and offer appropriate assistance. It is easier to walk on water when you can see your leader standing in front of you, holding out his or her hand.

5: Create a Return-and-Report Accountability System

I've already mentioned the importance of an accountability system. But it is so critical to delegation that it deserves more reinforcement here.

The Lord held Peter accountable for his shortcomings, lovingly helping him to learn from his mistakes and develop into the superb leader that the senior Apostle would eventually become. This concept of effective stewardship is taught in the scriptures and demonstrated by the Savior: "And he called him, and said unto him, How is it that I hear this of thee? give an account of thy stewardship; for thou mayest be no longer steward" (Luke 16:2). And, "For it is required of the Lord, at the hand of every steward, to render an account of his stewardship, both in time and in eternity" (D&C 72:3). The Lord also taught the importance of this principle in the parable of the talents (see Luke 19:20–26).

Remember, the Lord never punished Peter for his missteps. Peter was hard enough on himself. Can't you feel his regret and disappointment when he "[wept] bitterly" at his failures to acknowledge the Lord he loves or fails to meet His expectations? But Peter's disappointment is instructional and transformative. The return-and-report function of delegation serves that purpose. It is never a place for harsh words but for Christlike instruction and support—and when a task is well accomplished, for positive acknowledgement and appropriate praise.

I once served with a stake president who had the philosophy that an important part of his role was to "catch people doing something good." I saw the smiles and feelings of accomplishment those within his stewardship had when at the end of a return-and-report activity that he would say, sometimes with tears of appreciation in his eyes, "Well done. I believe the Lord would be pleased with your work."

6: Avoid Reassuming the Delegated Responsibility

We only see the Lord taking back delegated authority for unworthiness, not weak performance. Peter was never removed from the apostleship for his missteps. And we have no record of the Lord ever saying, "Never mind, Peter. I'll just do it Myself." What would Peter have learned from that?

Elder M. Russell Ballard explained why a delegated responsibility should not be reassumed by a leader, even in the case of a failure to perform:

> There is a difference between being responsible for getting the work done and doing the work yourself. For example, gone should be the days when

the elders quorum president feels he needs to personally finish the home teaching visits that others have missed. The same is true for Relief Society presidents with respect to visiting teaching. . . . Assignments should be made, responsibilities should be delegated, and members should be allowed to fulfill their stewardship as best they can. Counsel, advise, persuade, motivate—but don't do the work for them. Allow others to progress and grow, even if it means sometimes getting less-than-perfect results on the reports. ("O Be Wise")

President Dieter F. Uchtdorf explained that this is especially important when leading youth: "Leaders may be inclined to conduct, provide the music, or pray at a youth fireside or other meeting, but they should be 'shadow leaders,' overseeing the youth who perform these functions. This can be a challenge for parents and leaders because they know that they can probably do it faster or better. It takes patience to let the youth do it. Sometimes that involves letting them stumble" ("Tending the Flock: Teaching Leadership Skills to Youth").

Summary

I opened this chapter by relating my humbling experience of becoming a bishop. You may be interested to know that I did serve with three counselors, just as I had been prompted. And the Lord allowed me to serve, despite my rigorous travel schedule by blessing me with a significant decrease in travel without any reduction in my ability to provide for my family or negative effect on our business—a miracle my wife and I still cannot explain. Six months prior to my release, the travel resumed and normalized as it had before my call. This too, was miraculous to us, and a testimony that the Lord helps those He calls to serve with His delegated authority.

Delegation is critical for Church leaders because of the heaviness of the responsibilities of leadership and to develop future leaders. The Lord, as always, is a marvelous exemplar of these techniques and demonstrates effective delegation with the great Apostle Peter and others, including how to use proper Church structure and authority, delegate out significant responsibility (not just minor tasks), be clear about the responsibility and its importance, demonstrate confidence that the person can accomplish his or her delegated responsibility, create a return-and-report accountability system, and avoid reassuming the delegated responsibility.

In the next chapter, we will review one of the thornier challenges associated with Church leadership: how to resolve conflicts.

CHAPTER THIRTEEN: HOW TO RESOLVE CONFLICTS

"For verily, verily I say unto you, he that hath the spirit of contention is not of me, but is of the devil, who is the father of contention, and he stirreth up the hearts of men to contend with anger, one with another. Behold, this is not my doctrine, to stir up the hearts of men with anger, one against another; but this is my doctrine, that such things should be done away" (3 Nephi 11:29–30)

*W*hen *Reenie and* I started up our consulting and training company, we contacted a number of potential clients to get their recommendations on how we should expand our training portfolio. We were a little surprised to see that the most common request was for training about conflict resolution. "Please help us," they would say, "learn how to overcome disagreements," "manage personality conflicts," "stop fights," or "heal rifts in our organization." Further investigation convinced us that some sort of conflict was *inevitable* in the workplace, and if teams were unable to successfully resolve it, organizational effectiveness—and sometimes even individual health and safety—would be compromised.

This is not a new problem and certainly not one limited to secular organizations. The Apostle Paul wrote to the Corinthians, "But if any man seem to be contentious, we have no such custom, neither the churches of God. Now in this that I declare unto you I praise you not, that ye come together not for the better, but for the worse. For first of all, when ye come together in the church, I hear that there be divisions among you; and I partly believe it" (1 Corinthians 11:16–18).

The most common use of the words *conflict* and *contention* in the scriptures are in conjunction with wars—the armed consequence of the extreme end of the continuum of disagreement. But the terms are also used elsewhere to describe more common historical problems in the Church, things like disagreements on Church procedures, practices, and doctrine. The Lord, for example, instructed, "And according as I have commanded you thus shall ye baptize. And there shall be no disputations among you, as there have hitherto been; neither shall there be disputations among you concerning the points of my doctrine, as there have hitherto been" (3 Nephi 11:28). Further, He declared, "And this I do that I may establish my gospel, that there may not be so much contention; yea, Satan doth stir up the hearts of the people to contention concerning the points of my doctrine; and in these things they do err, for they do wrest the scriptures and do not understand them" (D&C 10:63).

Fortunately, this type of doctrinal and procedural conflict has lessened over the years, as revelation has settled many of the disputes about the proper operation of the Church, bringing us closer to the ideal espoused by Paul, of having "one Lord, one faith, one baptism" (Ephesians 4:5). But many stakes, wards, and families still struggle with the pain, sorrow, and grief that accompanies other types of unresolved disagreement.

Some of these disputes have to do with status or jealousy. The Lord Himself had to deal with some of this with His disciples: "And there was also a strife among them, which of them should be accounted the greatest" (Luke 22:24).

Other conflicts come from the normal difficulties of life. What is to be done, for example, when the Young Men's and the Young Women's organizations can't agree on joint activities? How can arguments about building use be resolved? How does a visiting teacher help a sister who confides that perpetual personal conflict between her and her husband has put their marriage in jeopardy? How do parents calm the disruptive arguments between their teenage sons?

But how do we reach that miraculous state of peace described in 4 Nephi, where "there was *no contention* among all the people, in all the land" (4 Nephi 1:13; emphasis added)?

A Few Tips on Resolving Conflict

Brother Dyer often taught his students that the first step of resolving conflict was to understand what causes it. His experience indicated that *most* conflict originates from a single thing. Would you like to know what accounts for most of the conflicts that, unresolved, can ultimately result in splintered wards, shattered auxiliaries, and broken homes?

The technical answer is violated expectations. What that means is that one party thinks that the other party is going to do something, but the other party does something different. Think about it. When was the last time you felt conflicted about someone? Was it because you thought the young men were going to provide the refreshments for the joint activity but they didn't? Or you expected your son to help you and his mother with the dishes, but he plopped onto the couch to play video games instead? Or because you thought your home teacher was going to come and help you move, your wife was going to pick up the kids after school, your eldest was going to help you get the kids ready for church, or the family you visit teach was going to be appreciative of the cake you made, but something else happened? That's violated expectation. You thought that X was going to happen, but Y happened instead.

At this point, the conflict is small, and it is usually possible to resolve it through thoughtful discussion. But without discussion, these situations often grow into deeper conflict and contention. Sometimes people can become offended and even leave the Church as a result of what almost always starts as a small disappointment. And sometimes the results of unresolved conflict are even worse.

Remember the cautionary story of Thomas B. Marsh, who left the Church over borrowed milk? A disagreement about whether the milk his wife returned had sufficient cream in it to be of the same quality as what she had borrowed led to Elder Marsh, who was then serving as the president of the Quorum of the Twelve, not only apostatizing but also swearing out an affidavit that played a role in the development of Governor Lilburn Bogg's Mormon Extermination Order. The order forced fifteen thousand Saints to be driven from their homes in Missouri—many of whom suffered, and some of whom died as a result (see George A. Smith's "Discourse," *Deseret News*, April 16, 1856, 44).

Fortunately, Brother Marsh repented and rejoined the Church after nineteen years of anger and bitterness. But think of the tragedy that might have been avoided if a calm discussion about violated expectations had been able to resolve the conflict before it erupted into life-destroying contention.

Discuss Expectations

If violated expectations aren't discussed and resolved early, normal feelings of confusion, disappointment, or embarrassment often turn into secondary emotions such as resentment or anger. Once a secondary emotion is attached, the conflict starts a sort of pressurized fire inside us, and resolution becomes increasingly difficult.

Ironically, attempts to avoid the conflict by ignoring it or staying silent during these early stages may actually deepen the problem as the unresolved anger expands like lava bubbling inside of a volcano, waiting until its poisonous gas can no longer be contained. This is especially true if similar unresolved situations have occurred previously. The situations accumulate; building more and more pressure that requires some sort of venting to resolve safely. If the anger continues to build until it erupts uncontrollably, it causes compounding damage. If the eruption occurs internally, serious emotional or spiritual destruction can occur. If the eruption is external, hurtful words may be spewed that, upon reflection, the individual later wishes they could retract. People in the path of the eruption can be seriously burned, even if they had nothing to do with the original problem.

This is the method Satan encourages to cause maximum suffering by stirring up people's hearts to feel things such as, "They are always letting me down like that," or, "I need to get even," or, "I'm right and they're wrong," or, "I need to hurt them like they hurt me." The Spirit departs. The light disappears. The dark steam of contention covers those affected like a blinding clouds of ash.

Instead, you might lovingly say something soon after the violated expectation occurs, such as, "Brother Weston, was I mistaken in assuming that the young men were going to bring the refreshments tonight? I felt disappointed we didn't have any." Or, "Son, didn't we agree that we'd do the dishes together? I feel sad when I see your mother doing them without you after she worked so hard to make us dinner." Or, "Brother Jones, did we have a miscommunication about our move? I felt a little let down when you didn't come over to help." Or, "Sweetheart, did I get mixed up about who was picking up the kids? I thought we agreed you were going to do it." Or, "Honey, can you help me with the kids, please? Remember how we talked about this in family home evening?" Or, "Sister Chang, the reason I dropped the cake by was to let you know I was thinking about you, and I'm worried that I might have unintentionally offended you because of it. I'm sorry."

Once the expectation is expressed, several things can happen. First, you might find that your expectation was never communicated properly. It is not fair to hold someone else accountable for anything they didn't know you expected of them. ("Sorry, Honey, I didn't know I was supposed to pick them up.") Second, you might discover that your expectation was understood differently than you intended. ("Oops. I thought the move was next Thursday, not last Thursday. I feel really bad about that.") Third, you may come to understand that your expectation was communicated and understood but not agreed to. ("I thought you were just being nice when you said you'd bake me something. I'm gluten intolerant and didn't want a cake.") Fourth, you may come to understand that there are reasons for the expectation not being met. ("We totally forgot about the refreshments. Let us do them next time, okay?") Or fifth, you might find that the expectation was understood but the other party has exercised their agency and decided not to do what was expected of them. ("I didn't want to do the dishes.")

As a Christlike leader, you will learn from the first two instances to be more effective in setting and communicating expectations. From the third, you will learn that expectations need to be realistic and agreed upon to be effective. From the fourth, you'll learn compassion and patience. And from the fifth, you will learn how to teach, correct, and forgive. Your positive personal experiences dealing with conflict situations will enable you to help others with them as well. And if you—as most of us do from time to time—find that you waited until after a full-fledged-lava-spewing-conflict occurred to resolve it, you can teach others from your experience how repenting can cleanse the soul.

Find Common Ground

In our professional responsibilities, we have been called on to help resolve deep-seated conflict between labor and management, organizational functions, or powerful feuding managers. Honestly, in these types of deep, long-lasting conflict, there is nothing we know off that can guarantee a successful resolution of the conflict every time. Sometimes talking about violated expectations helps, and other times it is too late for that.

But those times we have seen an effective resolution, the people have been able to agree on some type of common ground—a shared objective that superseded their differences and allowed them to do the difficult and humbling work of reconciliation. So we too must find a reason as Church leaders to help those suffering from conflict to rise above their differences to heal our wards, auxiliaries, and homes.

A wise leader helps those struggling with conflict to find that shared objective. As a bishop, I had many discussions with couples in peril. I would often ask, "What is a goal you can both agree to work toward?" Some would say, "Save our marriage." Others: "do whatever we can to help our children," "eliminate contention and restore the harmony in our home," or "become ready to be sealed in the temple." Those who could find a mutually agreeable goal were often successful in the difficult tasks of resolving their differences. Those who couldn't agree on a shared goal were seldom successful.

One good goal for those in conflict is a common love of the Savior and a desire to live by His teachings and follow His perfect example.

That can help people overcome enormous personal differences and difficulties.

How the Lord Resolved Conflict

Through the Lord's personal example, we learn much about how to resolve conflict. One example of this can be found after the Lord concluded praying in the Garden of Gethsemane that the cup of His atoning sacrifice might pass from Him. Imagine what it must have been like to stand in the garden when "a great multitude with swords and staves, from the chief priests and the scribes and the elders" (Mark 14:43) came to capture and imprison Jesus for capital crimes He, as the only sinless one, could not have committed. As Judas approached, "Jesus said unto him, Friend, wherefore art thou come? Then came they, and laid hands on Jesus, and took him" (Matthew 26:50).

Notice here how the Savior attempted to diffuse the situation by using words such as *friend*, despite the fact that He spoke to a betrayer. His confronters outnumbered His followers, clearly had evil designs, and carried weapons. I have to assume with these wording choices that the Master also used a calm and comforting tone of voice, even though the multitude probably assaulted ("laid hands on") Him.

The affront on the Savior was too much for Peter who, in the heat of the conflict, flashed his sword and severed the right ear of Malchus, the servant of the high priest (see John 18:7–12): "And Jesus answered and said, Suffer ye thus far. And he touched his ear, and healed him" (Luke 22:51).

I wonder how many of us would display compassion for someone who was threatening our life, as Malchus did the Savior? The Garden healing is a remarkable example of forgiveness and charity—the true love of Christ. How many conflicts could be resolved if each party thought less about their own pain and more about the wounds of their enemies?

Matthew's account added this kind but firm rebuke of Peter: "Then said Jesus unto him, Put up again thy sword into his place: for all they that take the sword shall perish with the sword" (Matthew 26:52), suggesting that confronting violence with violence is not His approved method of dealing with conflict.

How did the Savior resolve the conflict once it had escalated to physical violence? Did He fight back? No. He healed the ear of one of His attackers. He displayed compassion rather than anger, self-control rather than rage. But He still bravely stood His ground, asking those who attacked Him why they hadn't tried to capture Him earlier in a public setting, probably pricking their hearts for the cowardly method of approaching Him under the cloaking cover of darkness (Luke 22:52–53). The Lord, ever the master teacher of morality, risked a provocation of His armed oppressors with His response.

He had the power to extricate Himself, but He didn't use it because this conflict was part of what was required of Him by the Father. He explained, "Thinkest thou that I cannot now pray to my Father, and he shall presently give me more than twelve legions of angels? But how then shall the scriptures be fulfilled, that thus it must be?" (Matthew 26:53–54).

In John's account, we read, "Jesus answered, I have told you that I am he: if therefore ye seek me, let these go their way: That the saying might be fulfilled, which he spake, Of them which thou gavest me have I lost none" (John 18:8–9).

I include this part of the story to emphasize that the Lord negotiated with His captors to free His friends because He wanted the disciples to be safe. I have counseled people who thought it was necessary for them to remain, for example, in physically or emotionally abusive situations, convincing themselves somehow that the Christlike thing to do in the midst of their conflict was to endure further (unnecessary) suffering as a way to "turn the other cheek," or display forgiveness for their tormentors.

I believe this example from the last days of the Savior's life demonstrates that the Lord does not expect us to do anything of that sort. Abuse in the home or the Church cannot be tolerated, and God's harshest punishments are reserved for those who abuse children or others who are weak. He expects His followers to be safe and to protect themselves (and those depending on them) from avoidable harm. Forgiving others simply means that we will leave judgment to God and not carry that burden on our own mortal shoulders. But it never requires us to compromise our safety or the safety of others in our care. Similarly,

Church leaders shouldn't feel that they should substitute for the police, mental health professionals, or soldiers during conflict situations more appropriately suited to those with special training and responsibilities.

Conflict-Resolution Methods Displayed by the Savior

From this account, we can extrapolate additional tips for resolving conflict situations as the Lord would.

First, remain calm. In conflict situations, use soothing words and tone.

Second, don't lower yourself to the tactics of others. The Lord didn't call down avenging angels even though He was unjustly attacked and accused. He didn't fight back with the weapons used against Him either, even though those around Him had some and felt it was a justifiable response.

Third, don't escalate the conflict. Though it is difficult to not lash out when we are angry, the Lord's way is to display patience, long-suffering, and personal control. He tried to diffuse the situation rather than escalating it. He is a peacemaker.

Fourth, strive to heal those with whom you are in conflict. Demonstrate compassion and sympathy for their pain. Anybody can love their friends, but the Lord taught, "Love your enemies, bless them that curse you, do good to them that hate you, and pray for them which despitefully use you, and persecute you" (Matthew 5:44).

Fifth, stand up for yourself bravely in a firm and loving manner. And sixth, don't place yourself in harm's way.

If I were a bishop, elders quorum president, or Scoutmaster again, I think I might read over this story of the Savior in the Garden of Gethsemane with someone I was counseling with about a conflict and discuss together how His approach might be useful. I might ask questions such as, "How did the Lord handle this situation? What can we learn from this scripture about resolving our disagreements and conflicts? How can this apply to you?"

The Gadianton Robber Solution

I think there is a story in the Book of Mormon that is instructive when discussing conflict. As you will recall, the Gadianton robbers were the nemeses of the Nephite people. Helaman observed, "And behold, in the end of this book ye shall see that this Gadianton did prove the overthrow, yea, almost the entire destruction of the people of Nephi" (Helaman 2:13).

Both the Nephite and Lamanite nations struggled mightily with these outlaws in armed conflict, and the Lamanites finally found the only way to destroy them: "And it came to pass that the Lamanites did hunt the band of robbers of Gadianton; and they did preach the word of God among the more wicked part of them, insomuch that this band of robbers was utterly destroyed from among the Lamanites" (Helaman 6:37).

This is the ultimate and only sustainable solution to all conflict. If those in conflict become converted—experiencing the change of heart that is possible for the true follower of Jesus Christ—all contention disappears. This is what we strive to achieve in the Church. Until that time, however, the only respite from conflict in the secular world is found in the peaceful souls of those who follow the teachings of the Lord explicitly.

Summary

Though in this world it is unlikely that we will ever achieve a complete elimination of conflict and contention, there is much we can do to reduce it in the Church. Understanding that conflict is often caused by violated expectations and can be reduced by openly and honestly discussing these violations soon after they occur is a key insight. And finding common ground is also useful, especially a shared goal between the parties in conflict that is equally desirable to everyone, allowing them to rise above their individual concerns and do the difficult work of reconciliation.

The capture of the Savior in the Garden of Gethsemane offers additional insight into how Christlike leaders can deal with difficult conflict situations: Remain calm, don't lower yourself to the tactics of others, don't escalate the conflict, strive to heal those with whom you are in conflict, stand up for yourself bravely in a firm and loving manner, and don't place yourself in harm's way.

Ultimately, however, the key to the elimination of conflict is teaching and living the full gospel of Jesus Christ. An attribute of the truly converted is an absence of conflict and contention. Blessed is the ward or home that discovers this. As the Savior taught in the Sermon on the Mount: "Blessed are the peacemakers: for they shall be called the children of God" (Matthew 5:9).

CHAPTER FOURTEEN: HOW TO HELP PEOPLE DEAL WITH TRIALS AND TRAGEDY

"Bear one another's burdens, that they may be light; Yea, and . . .
mourn with those that mourn; yea, and comfort those that stand
in need of comfort" (Mosiah 18:8–9)

*A*s we moved around from city to city, following our careers
and serving in the Church, Reenie and I struggled privately
with a life-altering personal trial. At first, our inability to
have children seemed like a temporary setback we felt sure Father
in Heaven would correct. We prayed unceasingly. We requested and
received numerous blessings and demonstrated our faith in these
blessings through works as well, dedicating significant time, effort,
and resources to obtaining the finest medical assistance available. We
both underwent surgeries. We participated in expensive treatments
that took us within a breath of losing our emotional well-being.

But nothing worked. As it became increasingly evident that for
some undiscoverable reason we would likely never conceive, even our
efforts to adopt children were thwarted. Our discouragement turned
into depression and grief for the loss of the children and grandchildren
we would not know in this life.

Eventually, we had the blessing of spiritual healing and renewed
faith in our Heavenly Father's childless plan for us in mortality. But
we had many years of barely survivable sadness leading up to the day
that He, in His infinite compassion, lifted our pain away.

Sometimes Members Make It Worse

During the darkest decade of these times, well-intended Church members sometimes increased rather than decreased our sorrow. Many asked us why we were waiting to start a family, assuming that we were postponing this decision in favor of our successful careers. We confided in our closest friends, but the pain was so great for us at the time that we preferred to politely extricate ourselves from these other discussions without explanation. Afterward, my sweet wife would usually dissolve into tears.

The family focus of the gospel often made us feel incomplete and inadequate. Talks and testimonies about children stabbed at us like spears. We found it difficult to teach or even participate in the frequent lessons on parenthood or raising families. Mother's and Father's Day were so unbearable that we searched for reasons to be out of town and away from our ward on those days. Holidays, Primary programs, and even hearing children laugh in the hallways were all difficult. Once when a leader asked us to stay and clean up after a ward activity—so that "the people with children could enjoy their evening out together"—we briefly discussed whether we should stop coming to church for a season. We felt so alone.

Why Do We Have Trials and Tribulations?

Later, we would look back on this time as our own Zion's camp, a difficult but powerful preparation for a number of leadership callings that required us to have the sort of empathy and compassion that seldom comes without deep personal suffering. We rediscovered the essential nature of the focus on families in Church services. But at the time, we often asked, "Why us?"

We were not as mature as a neighbor of ours who suffered and died from a rare brain disease, leaving his wife and two young children. At his funeral, we heard of a time when his sweetheart tearfully asked him, "Why did this have to happen to you? You're such a good man." To which, he answered, "Why not me? I'm no better than anybody else." He recalled the trials of Job, whom the Lord loved.

There isn't a branch or ward in the Church where people aren't suffering from trials and tribulations—often silently. The reality of our mortal probation is that the refining process of perfection inevitably requires periodic scalding pains of disappointment, illness, betrayal, loss, and grief. It is such a predictable part of the human experience that Alma spoke of bearing one another's burdens, mourning with those who mourn, and comforting those who stand in need of comfort as being a basic responsibility of all who will be baptized into the Church (as noted in the scripture that opened this chapter). It's important to note that Alma didn't ask us to try to *eliminate* the burdens of others, *shorten* their mourning, or help people *avoid* needing comforting in the first place. We try, of course, to help each other dodge the avoidable suffering that comes from personal sin or a lack of preparation and skills, but we realize that there will still be unavoidable pain that results from the sins of others or from the inevitable trials and tragedies of life. That is an inescapable and important part of this mortal existence.

Dealing with Real Challenges

How does an elders quorum president really help a brother who lost his job and feels worthless to his family? What do you say to the mother of five whose husband has abandoned them, or to a couple who feel betrayed by the poor choices of their children? How do you help a father struggling with addiction? What does a young, single Relief Society president say to provide comfort to a family mourning the loss of a child? How does a Primary presidency help a child cope with her mother's terminal illness? How do leaders of the Young Men help youth who are acting out rebelliously because of an imminent divorce of their parents?

Even experienced leaders can feel dwarfed beside the monumental challenges that frequently loom over people as part of their mortal probationary experience. We are blessed to live in a day when many medical professionals, counselors, and government programs can provide meaningful assistance, but challenges for Church leaders who long to reach out to their brothers and sisters in distress remains great, even daunting at times.

While I served as a bishop, for example, a dear family in our ward found their unconscious eighteen-month-old daughter in a neighbor's pond. I ached so deeply for them, but I wasn't sure what to do. As their leader, I wanted to make things better and take away the excruciating pain of their sorrow, and yet I knew that I couldn't do that. So what should I say to help them? How could I provide hope or solace? How could I comfort them? I spent hours praying for guidance. And then the answer came.

How Can We Help?

All I could do was love them. Spend some time. Help them plan. Feed them. Be there if they couldn't tolerate solitude. Leave if they needed to be alone. Fast. Pray. Read scriptures with them if they desired it. Clean their house.

I realized that healing would come from the Lord, not me. There was no way to fix it, no amazing words to say. I just needed to be present with them and let them know that people cared.

We organized a vigil of families to line the hospital halls all day and all night until the little angel girl slipped beyond her mortal binding a few days later. Mainly, we shed quiet tears together. We sang hymns. There was a lot of hugging and many meals. No attempts to answer the unanswerable why. We just mourned along with them. We put a few more shoulders under their burdens to make them bearable. We provided some comfort. The Relief Society president and I helped them plan a funeral, and when it was time, we all had a bittersweet memorial service together. This tragedy pulled us all closer together. It bound us together as a ward and as friends in a way that I believe is eternal. The healing continues to this day.

In this chapter, I'd like to suggest some ways that a Christlike leader can help people with their trials and tribulations. First, I'll review a variety of resources that can help in various times of need. Second, I'd like to suggest some things to avoid—leadership words or actions that, while well-intended, may actually hurt more than they help. Third, I'll discuss how properly understanding the doctrine of prayer can help us with life challenges. Fourth, I'll discuss the enabling power of the Atonement and suggest how this doctrine can bring great comfort to the sick and weary. Often, the Christlike leader finds that the most helpful thing he or she can do is to help others turn to the Savior for solace. He alone is able to bind certain wounds.

Let's discuss each of these four tools for helping others in need in more detail. After that, let's review how, during His mortal ministry, the Lord used visits, scriptures, and prayers to comfort others.

Helpful Resources

Some trials can be aided with Church resources. Many financial or health challenges that come from a lack of education or self-reliance skills, for example, can be minimized by teaching Relief Society and priesthood lessons on topics such as proper diet, food preparation, hygiene, and other inspired welfare principles that assist Church members in being physically, financially, emotionally, mentally, and spiritually healthy.

Primary and youth classes and activities can help children and young men and women understand family interaction skills, the Word of Wisdom, morality, and preparation to become productive members of society. These types of topics are woven throughout the approved curriculum and can be supplemented with activities such as stake preparedness fairs that teach budgeting, food storage, and emergency preparation or fifth-Sunday activities that teach a variety of basic life and sin-avoidance skills. Ward or auxiliary service projects can also help others who are in need and teach potential employment or home, yard, or vehicle maintenance skills. A Christlike leader knows those in his or her stewardship well enough to suggest potential activities to the ward or stake councils that will address real needs for real people. These councils can also address how programs like home and visiting teaching can bless the lives of others.

Bishops and Relief Society presidents can also help people in need receive assistance from the fast offering resources of the Church. These sacred funds are used to sustain life—not lifestyle—and need to be administered according to the CHI so that they bless lives instead of creating debilitating dependencies. Some areas of the Church are blessed with other resources as well, such as access to bishop's storehouses, Deseret Industries, employment centers, and Perpetual Education funding.

As a bishop, I was especially grateful for the Family Social Services in our area. Counseling resources were useful for many members of our ward who had addiction, marriage, emotional, or mental health challenges, and who appreciated having practical guidance from someone with a gospel background. If you want to know what resources are available in your area for those you lead, check with your bishop. Bishops can learn more about these resources from their stake presidents and from the bishop's welfare council, which should also be current on appropriate government assistance programs in their area. Church websites are also helpful.

There are certain challenges, however, that these resources may not be useful for. In those cases, the rule of thumb—to paraphrase the Hippocratic oath taught to medical practitioners—is to "do no harm."

What Doesn't Help

We had learned from our own experience that weak attempts to offer solace to someone struggling with a trial by saying things such as, "I know how you feel," "everything will be okay," or "I'm sure there is a reason for this" felt hollow and unhelpful. These sorts of comments even seemed to demean or trivialize our personal struggle. We knew that to others, our experience might seem insignificant. But it didn't feel like that to us, and well-intended efforts to "fix" or "explain" things usually made it worse. Consider Figure 14-1 for more examples of the dos and don'ts of comforting others.

Figure 14-1: Tips for Comforting Others

Do	Don't
• offer condolences	• say you get how they feel
• offer service (to bring a meal or help with the kids or stay in the home during the funeral)	• ignore them just because you can't think of a specific way you can help
• share a scripture	• give them a lecture or tell them their trials are part of God's plan (unless you have a specific prompting to do so)
• offer to pray for or with them	
• share your experiences if they are relevant (if you lost your mother too, had cancer, had a wayward child, and so on)	
	• tell them it will all be okay
• show empathy	• share your experiences if they aren't relevant
• get them helpful resources	• minimize struggles or concerns
• be loving	• make them feel needy
	• be judgmental

One of our most comforting experiences came, oddly enough, from a friend who started but could not continue one of the many blessings we requested. "I'm so sorry," he said. "I'm just not getting any impressions. I can't continue." There was something about a worthy priesthood holder who was so close to the Spirit that he was unwilling to say what he knew we wanted to hear that reassured us that our trial was known by the Lord and apparently necessary for our own good. We realized at that time that we would not have our hoped-for miracle but that our prayers were still being answered by Father in Heaven. It wasn't the answer we wanted, but it was full of love and the promise of the strength to endure our trial.

Why the Answer to Some Prayers Is No

Though it is difficult for someone in the midst of a trial to understand, our experience taught us that sometimes the answer to prayer has to be no. We err when we say to ourselves or others that our prayers aren't being answered simply because we don't get the answer we hoped for. Heavenly Father's answer was no, even to his Only Begotten's prayer about letting the cup pass. That's an answer.

Sometimes our Father has to respond to our pleading with something like this, "I'm sorry, my little one. But there is a reason that I cannot give you the answer [or relief or blessing] you desire. For your own good, and because I love you, and I know what is best for you now and in eternity, the answer to your prayer is no."

Many of us have witnessed miracles. We, for example, saw a miraculous cure of a young father's cancer as a result of a ward fast. Several lives were extended in ways that were medically inexplicable. I still recall a sweet Primary child saying, "We did it! We fasted, and a miracle happened. We should do this for everybody."

But these marvelous manifestations are called miracles precisely because they are *not* the norm. If our Father removed or corrected every difficulty of mortality, the purpose of life would be obviated. How can there be meaningful choice in the absence of difficult options? How can we prove ourselves without struggle? How do we build spiritual strength without having to do the exercise associated with lifting heavy burdens? Without illness and opposition, how do we learn gratitude for our blessings? Humility? Patience? How do we finally learn to submit our will to the Father's?

The purpose of life is not to escape burdens but rather to learn how to bear them.

The Enabling Power of the Atonement

Thankfully, for most of us, the greatest of our trials and tribulations are for but a season. And we can take solace in the fact that there is always one person who has been through more difficult trials than we will ever endure: our Savior, Jesus Christ. He can have perfect empathy for our pains and sufferings. He alone can whisper, "I understand what you are going through." Perhaps the best thing a Christlike leader can do for others in their trials and tribulations is help them rely on the Lord to sustain them through their most difficult times.

In Alma, we read, "And he shall go forth, *suffering pains and afflictions and temptations of every kind*; and this that the word might be fulfilled which saith he will take upon him the *pains and the sicknesses* of his people. And he will take upon him death, that he may loose the bands of death which bind his people; and *he will take upon him their infirmities*, that his bowels may be filled with mercy, according to the flesh, that he may know according to the flesh how to succor his people according to their infirmities" (Alma 7:11–12; emphasis added). This is also reinforced in Matthew 8:17: "That it might be fulfilled which was spoken by Esaias the prophet, saying, Himself took our infirmities, and bare our sicknesses."

Note how the scripture in Alma in particular clarifies that the Atonement covers not only redemption from sin and death but also the power to endure pains, afflictions, sicknesses, and infirmities. Which ones? "Every kind." The Lord has empathy for every pain, affliction, sickness, and infirmity because, in a way that we cannot comprehend, He has suffered them all. And His Atonement promises strength for us to endure them too.

What about the pain of cancer, third-degree burns, or Alzheimer's? Of course. Mental illness? The death of a spouse or child? Being a caretaker of someone you love who is suffering? Slavery? Abuse? Yes, all of them. For every possible pain a human can suffer, for every possible affliction and sickness, He has been there before us. We can lean on Him for understanding and strength. The enabling power of the Atonement can help us endure what we must.

Of this magnificent power, Elder David A. Bednar said,

The Savior has suffered not just for our iniquities but also for the inequality, the unfairness, the pain, the anguish, and the emotional distresses that so frequently beset us. There is no physical pain, no anguish of soul, no suffering of spirit, no infirmity or weakness that you or I ever experience during our mortal journey that the Savior did not experience first. You and I in a moment of weakness may cry out, "No one understands. No one knows." No human being, perhaps, knows. But the Son of God perfectly knows and understands, for He felt and bore our burdens before we ever did. And because He paid the ultimate price and bore that burden, He has perfect empathy and can extend to us His arm of mercy in so many phases of our life. He can reach out, touch, succor—literally run to us—and strengthen us to be more than we could ever be and help us to do that which we could never do through relying upon only our own power. ("The Atonement and the Journey of Mortality," *Ensign*, April 2012)

As leaders, we can help people learn to lay their burdens at the feet of the Lord and engage the enabling power of the Atonement. Even the prophet Joseph had to learn how to do this.

The Trials of Joseph

When the Prophet Joseph reached an extremity of suffering after months of relentless incarceration in the Liberty Jail, he cried out, "O God, where art thou? And where is the pavilion that covereth thy hiding place? How long shall thy hand be stayed, and thine eye, yea thy pure eye, behold from the eternal heavens the wrongs of thy people and of thy servants, and thine ear be penetrated with their cries?" (D&C 121:1–2).

Then came the answer: "My son, peace be unto thy soul; thine adversity and thine afflictions shall be but a small moment; And then, if thou endure it well, God shall exalt thee on high; thou shalt triumph over all thy foes" (D&C 121:7–8). The answer continued in D&C 122:

If thou art called to pass through tribulation; if thou art in perils among false brethren; if thou art in perils among robbers; if thou art in perils by land or by sea; If thou art accused with all manner of false accusations; if thine enemies fall upon thee; if they tear thee from the society of thy father and mother and brethren and sisters; and if with a drawn sword thine enemies tear thee from the bosom of thy wife, and of thine offspring. . . . And if thou shouldst be cast into the pit, or into the hands of murderers, and the sentence of death passed upon thee; if thou be cast into the deep . . . if the very jaws of hell shall gape open the mouth wide after thee, know thou, my son, that all these things shall give thee experience, and shall be for thy good. The Son of Man hath descended below them all. Art thou greater than he? (D&C 122:5–8)

As leaders, we may not be able to take away the pain and suffering that accompanies the trials of this life. But we can point people to the One who can. Through the enabling power of the Atonement, it is possible to endure all that is necessary for us to complete our mortal probation. And with the promised comforting power of the Holy Ghost, we can endure it well.

Now, let us see what else the Lord's mortal ministry teaches us about comforting others.

How the Lord Helped People with Trials

It seems that the Lord spent much of His ministry helping people with their trials and tribulations. We'll explore this in greater detail in a later chapter about shepherding. But for this chapter, suffice it to say that He healed, wept, and comforted.

Different Types of Healing

The Lord healed many who were sick or afflicted in body or spirit. There are times when, according to the will of God, we too can be instruments of miraculous healing through the worthy use of prayer and priesthood blessings that call down the powers of heaven.

But there are other times when a trial is one that is critical for the eternal development of a soul, when a death is appointed, and when our loving Father desires that we work through the difficulty, handicap, or hardship to perfect ourselves or others. These times call for a different kind of healing.

When the father who lost his eighteen-month-old daughter bravely spoke at the fast and testimony meeting following her passing, he said something like this: "We did not have the miracle we hoped for, but we did witness a miracle. It was the miracle of you reaching out to love and comfort us in our time of sorrow. It was the miracle of your support and friendship. It did not heal our daughter, but it is helping to heal us."

Jesus Wept

As leaders, we can follow the Savior's example in the other ways of comforting those in need of comfort. When Lazarus, the brother of Martha and Mary fell gravely ill, the Lord was apprised of the tribulation facing those He loved so dearly. The Lord knew before His disciples did, however, that the news was worse than what they thought. Lazarus had actually died: "He saith unto them, Our friend Lazarus sleepeth; but I go, that I may awake him out of sleep. Then said his disciples, Lord, if he sleep, he shall do well. Howbeit Jesus spake of his death: but they thought that he had spoken of taking of rest in sleep. Then said Jesus unto them plainly, Lazarus is dead" (John 11:11–14).

By the time the Lord arrived at the home of Martha and Mary, "he found that . . . [Lazarus] had lain in the grave four days already" (John 11:17).

The sisters came out and met the Lord. "Then when Mary was come where Jesus was, and saw him, she fell down at his feet, saying unto him, Lord, if thou hadst been here, my brother had not died. When Jesus therefore saw her weeping, and the Jews also weeping which came with her, he groaned in the spirit, and was troubled, And said, Where have ye laid him? They said unto him, Lord, come and see" (John 11:32–34).

And then we have the shortest yet one of the most powerful verses in the scriptures: "Jesus wept" (John 11:35).

Why are these two words allowed to stand alone as a verse of scripture? I believe it is because they convey a poignant example of how to mourn with those who mourn. He didn't preach or lecture; He just wept. The Lord already knew that He would raise His friend Lazarus from the dead, but out of respect and love for His friends and the mourners, He first shared in the grieving process with them, causing observers to proclaim, "Behold how he loved him!" (John 11:36).

Not until then did He perform the miracle: "And . . . he cried with a loud voice, Lazarus, come forth. And he that was dead came forth, bound hand and foot with graveclothes: and his face was bound about with a napkin. Jesus saith unto them, Loose him, and let him go" (John 11:43–44).

Providing Christlike Comfort through
Visits, Scriptures, and Prayers

For those the Lord did not heal, such as the rich young man who chose not to sell all that he had to give to the poor and become a disciple, the Lord still provided evidence of caring. He shared clear and saving doctrine. With others, He shared the guidance and solace of scriptures. His mere presence was a comfort to many others who sought only to be near Him. He prayed for those in the New World who loved Him but were mourning His too-brief visit and imminent departure. He even prayed from the cross for those afflicted with the job of killing Him: "Then said Jesus, Father, forgive them; for they know not what they do. And they parted his raiment, and cast lots" (Luke 23:34).

By visiting, sharing scriptures, and praying, we can follow the Lord's example of comforting those with trials and tribulations. Some of my most powerful and sweet sessions with those I tried to comfort as a bishop came from sitting down together, reading scriptures about the Atonement or the plan of salvation, and praying jointly. This has been helpful to me as a home teacher and husband too.

Summary

There are many types of trials and tribulations that are part of the mortal experience. Some, such as financial struggles or the challenges of undereducation, can be aided through the inspired programs of the Church such as fast offerings, perpetual education programs, and emergency preparedness instruction.

But there are many tragedies that money and education cannot rectify. The Lord showed us how to help people with these trials through healing, tears, and comforting actions such as visiting, sharing scriptures, and praying. It is a blessing to know that the enabling power of His Atonement can help us and those we serve with the power to endure the trials that cannot be removed. An understanding of the doctrine of why these trials are necessary can put things into a more eternal, manageable perspective.

Our personal experiences as leaders will teach us empathy, tolerance, patience, and love, helping us be more effective as we assist others in their times of need. And we will learn that sometimes the most powerful way to help others isn't with words but rather with our quiet presence and simple service offerings such as dinners, babysitting, and cleaning as a demonstration of Christlike love.

Reenie and I came to understand, through our own trials, that the Lord knows and loves us. We are stronger and better people as a result. We have a testimony that we will have children in the next life, with any luck, as Reenie says, "when there is a better alternative than changing diapers."

But until then, Church service has blessed us with the opportunity to develop wonderful relationships with many families and children, a blessing we would not have realized if we had succumbed to the temptation of inactivity as a way to lessen our pain. Our leadership roles have also blessed us with opportunities to forget ourselves in service, and now, as we get older, the callings that once held great anguish for us provide the greatest comfort and promise. We love, for example, opportunities of serving in the nursery. It has become clear to us that though Church leaders can't alleviate all of the suffering that comes from mortal trials, the Lord can. And in time, because of the Atonement and gospel of Jesus Christ, all will be well.

Next, let's review how to avoid unrighteous dominion.

CHAPTER FIFTEEN: HOW TO AVOID UNRIGHTEOUS DOMINION

"We have learned by sad experience that it is the nature and disposition of almost all men, as soon as they get a little authority, as they suppose, they will immediately begin to exercise unrighteous dominion" (D&C 121:39)

*D*uring the part of our careers when Reenie and I worked in human resources assignments with Procter and Gamble and Tektronix, we sometimes heard some complaints from employees about a leader who had said or done something wrong. These reports were especially troubling when they involved actions that were dominating, controlling, or even emotionally abusive.

The effects of these leadership errors were significant, often reducing morale, slashing productivity, and decimating trust across large swaths of the afflicted organization. Both companies were swift to deal with these problems, and if the leaders were unable to make the necessary modifications, they were removed from their positions.

A Common Mistake

As the scripture that opened this chapter suggests, unfortunately, unrighteous dominion is a tendency of "almost all men." I believe that it is a mistake I have personally made in some assignments, where—in my anxiety to do well or be efficient—I have been overly controlling or demanding. This is not good. It is not the Savior's way.

Unrighteous dominion can actually subvert the agency of others and lead to many forms of apostasy. It creates disease in the soul. It is a grievous sin. Some of the strongest admonitions in the scriptures warn against this abuse of authority. For example, in the Doctrine and Covenants, we read,

> The rights of the priesthood are inseparably connected with the powers of heaven, and . . . the powers of heaven cannot be controlled nor handled only upon the principles of righteousness. That they may be conferred upon us, it is true; but when we undertake to cover our sins, or to gratify our pride, our vain ambition, or to exercise control or dominion or compulsion upon the souls of the children of men, in any degree of unrighteousness, behold, the heavens withdraw themselves; the Spirit of the Lord is grieved; and when it is withdrawn, Amen to the priesthood or the authority of that man. (D&C 121:36–37)

Though this scripture specifically relates to priesthood authority, the principle applies to all leadership positions in the Church. Nevertheless, we see countless warnings for men in particular about avoiding unrighteous dominion as leaders in their homes.

Avoiding Unrighteous Dominion in Marriage

The doctrine of priesthood leadership of the home should never be used to justify unrighteous dominion. Elder Richard G. Scott of the Quorum of the Twelve taught, "In some cultures, tradition places a man in a role to dominate, control, and regulate all family affairs. That is not the way of the Lord. In some places the wife is almost owned by her husband, as if she were another of his personal possessions. That is a cruel, mistaken vision of marriage encouraged by Lucifer that every priesthood holder must reject. It is founded on the false premise that a man is somehow superior to a woman. Nothing could be farther from the truth" ("Honor the Priesthood and Use It Well," *Ensign*, November 2008).

In rejecting the mistaken notion that marriage is a hierarchical institution, Elder L. Tom Perry of the Quorum of the Twelve added, "There is not a president or a vice president in a family. The couple works together eternally for the good of the family. . . . They are on equal footing. They plan and organize the affairs of the family jointly and unanimously as they move forward" ("Fatherhood, an Eternal Calling," *Ensign*, May 2004).

Avoiding Unrighteous Dominion over Children

These same principles apply to the other members of our families as well. In the April 2012 general conference, for example, Elder Larry Y. Wilson of the Seventy shared the following personal example about potential unrighteous dominion over children: "Wise parents must weigh when children are ready to begin exercising their own agency in a particular area of their lives. But if parents hold on to all decision-making power and see it as their 'right,' they severely limit the growth and development of their children."

Elder Wilson went on to relate a story of how, after much discussion, they allowed their daughter Mary to make her own decision about playing in a soccer championship game on Sunday. Mary bent to the pressure placed on her by her coach and teammates and decided to play. He said,

> Now what were we to do? After further discussion and receiving reassurance from the Spirit, we did as we had promised and permitted her to carry out her choice to play. After the game ended, Mary slowly walked over to her waiting mother. "Oh, Mom," she said, "that felt awful. I never want to feel like that again. I'm never playing another game on the Sabbath day." And she never did. Mary had now internalized the principle of Sabbath keeping. If we had forced her not to play the game, we would have deprived her of a precious and powerful learning experience with the Spirit." ("Only upon the Principles of Righteousness," *Ensign*, May 2012)

What Causes Unrighteous Dominion?

In our executive coaching work with business and government leaders, we often uncover that the reason they try to dominate or control others comes from a belief that they are superior to those they lead. Shockingly, this can even happen in the Church, regardless of how clearly inconsistent this assumption is with the Lord's teachings.

Renowned Christian author C. S. Lewis warned,

> It is a serious thing to live in a society of possible gods and goddesses, to remember that the dullest and most uninteresting person you can talk to may one day be a creature which, if you saw it now, you would be strongly tempted to worship . . . it is with the awe and the circumspection

proper to them, that we should conduct all our dealings with one another, all friendships, all loves, all play, all politics. There are no ordinary people. You have never talked to a mere mortal. Nations, cultures, arts, civilizations—these are mortal, and their life is to ours as the life of a gnat. But it is immortals whom we joke with, work with, marry, snub, and exploit—immortal horrors or everlasting splendors. . . . Next to the Blessed Sacrament itself, your neighbor is the holiest object presented to your senses. (*The Weight of Glory* [New York: Collier Books, Macmillan Publishing, 1980], 18–19)

Tips for Avoiding Unrighteous Dominion over Others

Fortunately, the scriptures that warn us about the problems of unrighteous dominion over others also offer the solution. Later in the same section of the Doctrine and Covenants, we read, "No power or influence can or ought to be maintained . . . only by persuasion, by long-suffering, by gentleness and meekness, and by love unfeigned; by kindness, and pure knowledge, which shall greatly enlarge the soul without hypocrisy, and without guile" (D&C 121:41–42).

These attributes of the Christlike leader are called "the principles of righteousness" in verse 36. Let's examine them each in more detail.

The Principles of Righteousness

Consider some examples of how the principles of righteousness can be used in lieu of unrighteous dominion.

Persuasion—rather than trying to dominate, force, or control others, the Christlike leader uses persuasion to encourage them to use their agency in ways that offer them the full benefits of the gospel. Because the leader assumes the best of everyone, he or she realizes that even subtle coercion is unnecessary and instead appeals to what is good in people. Instead of saying, "Martha, you must obey the commandments," or, "Martha, I want you to do your visiting teaching next month," try, "Martha, I know that when you choose to obey the commandments [or visit the sisters you've been assigned] that the Lord will bless you." Sharing personal experiences, the teachings of the prophets, and the scriptures can be persuasive, especially when Martha can feel the Spirit confirm that what she is being told is true. But she should be encouraged to build her own testimony and pray for her own guidance as well.

Nothing is more persuasive than personal divine direction from the Master who leads us all.

Long-suffering—everyone makes mistakes, and how a leader reacts to them can make a big difference in someone's eternal progression. The Christlike leader respects other people's agency. Criticism, derision, and censure (in all of their forms, including ignoring others or offering them the "silent treatment") have no place. Teaching moments and discipline—when necessary—are never done in anger but with patience and calmness. Even repeated offenses are handled with love and understanding. The Christlike leader doesn't raise his or her voice, argue, or engage in contentious actions or speech. He or she would never physically or emotionally hurt anyone, regardless of the other person's actions or language. When a mistake is made, try saying something like, "I'm so sorry that didn't work out for you. What is your plan to avoid having to go through that again?" Never say, "Next time, please do what I asked you to do."

Gentleness and meekness—the Christlike leader doesn't give orders and isn't prideful. He or she offers counsel, suggestions, and recommendations. He or she doesn't believe that others are inferior in any way, recognizing that a leadership calling does not imply superiority. The leader serves others and sets an example. Instead of saying, "Why aren't you doing what we agreed you would do?" or, "Please be better organized," the Christlike leader says, "What help do you need from me?" He or she responds to requests for help cheerfully. He or she is mild, obedient, humble, and even-tempered. The Christlike leader may suggest ways to do something but is reluctant to impose his or her methods on others, choosing instead to encourage people to do what works best for them, as long as it is consistent with gospel teachings. He or she doesn't dominate conversations or decisions or try to get people to think or act in his or her preferred way.

Love unfeigned—the Christlike leader can offer unfeigned love because he or she has invested the time and effort necessary to know others. He or she prays for them regularly. He or she knows their names and families and actively serves them (knowing that love comes for those served). The Christlike leader assumes that other people have good reasons for doing what they do and genuinely cares about their ideas and concerns and listens carefully to them. He or she feels the joys and sorrows of others. Unfeigned love allows the leader to do the right thing even when it is difficult and motivates him or her to help in time of need. The Christlike leader does not pretend to care for others and will love even those who seem unlovable.

Kindness—the Christlike leader never demeans others and is always respectful. People leave interactions with such a leader feeling loved and accepted, not criticized or chastised. He or she is not harsh or intolerant but rather is polite, courteous, and thoughtful. When assignments are necessary, for example, the leader asks for help instead of demanding it. He or she listens carefully to people and demonstrates respect for their opinions, showing real empathy for others and always being willing to help.

Pure knowledge—the Christlike leader knows the gospel and uses doctrine, scriptures, and counsel from prophets more than personal opinion. He or she teaches by the Spirit. When in doubt about someone's gospel question, he or she doesn't guess about an answer but rather says, "Let me find out for you," and then provides the proper answer from the scriptures, Church leaders, or the CHI. He or she doesn't try to represent the opinion of others without checking with them first and getting their permission to share the information. The Christlike leader doesn't gossip or tolerate half or partial truths; when presiding at a meeting when incorrect doctrine is taught, he or she lovingly corrects it so that the misinterpretation is not allowed to go unchallenged.

Without hypocrisy—the Christlike leader does what he or she teaches others and sets an example of righteousness, thus inviting others to follow. When he or she makes a mistake, it is admitted to; when he or she falls short, forgiveness is sought after, even if it is from a child. The Christlike leader would never ask someone to do something he or she wouldn't do, saying, "Who can help me set up the chairs for stake conference?" instead of, "We need some volunteers to set up chairs." If he or she asks for people's opinions, he or she both listens and takes action on those opinions.

Without guile—there is no manipulation in the tactics of the Christlike leader. He or she would never try to force somebody to do something they are uncomfortable doing or use guilt as a method to change someone. He or she is not selectively truthful, sneaky, sly, nor crafty, rather choosing to be transparent and open and honest with others. He or she wouldn't try to trick someone into saying or doing anything or pretend to go along with something she disagrees with, nor would he or she maneuver a council decision to come out another way by pretending to be hurt or disappointed. If a confidence needs to be held, for example, a true leader wouldn't pretend not to know, but he or she would say something like, "I'm sorry, but I cannot break that confidence."

The promises for those who eschew unrighteous dominion and instead lead with the principles of righteousness are marvelous. In Doctrine and Covenants, we read, "The Holy Ghost shall be thy constant companion, and thy scepter an unchanging scepter of righteousness and truth; and thy dominion shall be an everlasting dominion, and without compulsory means it shall flow unto thee forever and ever" (D&C 121:46).

Questions to Ask Yourself

In our work, Reenie and I are often asked to provide methods that help leaders assess their effectiveness. The best way to do this, of course, is to ask those being led about what they think is working or not working relative to the leader's actions. But another useful tool is what we call a self-assessment. In that spirit, honestly consider the following questions to determine how much you use the principles of righteousness rather than the practices or assumptions associated with unrighteous dominion.

1. Do I place the needs of people over the needs of a project, program, or assignment?
2. Do I treat every encounter with others as though that person is a son or daughter of God?
3. Would others describe me as humble?
4. Do I respect the views of others, even if I disagree with them?
5. Do people leave interactions with me feeling loved?
6. Do I make requests or give orders?
7. Would people say I respect their agency?
8. Do I ever take credit for others' ideas?
9. Do I accept accountability for my mistakes?

10. Do I blame others when things go poorly?

11. Would others say I'm respectful and polite?

12. Would others say I'm supportive and encouraging?

13. Do I ever (even subtly) try to force people to do the right thing?

14. Do I offer assistance more than direction?

15. Would people say that I'm a good listener?

16. While others are speaking, am I thinking of other things or really listening?

17. Would people say I try to manipulate them?

18. Do I build on other's ideas and suggestions?

19. Do I say things that might be viewed as critical?

20. Do I show appreciation to others? How? Do they feel appreciated?

21. Do I ever withhold approval or love?

22. Do I look for the best in people?

23. Do I ever assume that people have bad intentions?

How the Lord Used Principles of Righteousness

As always, the Lord provides the perfect example of righteous leadership. Consider how He dealt with the traitor Judas. Did we hear Him chastise him? Withdraw His love? And even though He knew Judas's evil intentions, did He try to coerce him to change his plans, or try to trick him? The answer to all of these questions: no. Instead, we read of persuasion, long-suffering, gentleness and meekness, love unfeigned, kindness, and pure knowledge without hypocrisy or guile. We read in John:

> Now before the feast of the passover, when Jesus knew that his hour was come that he should depart out of this world unto the Father, having loved his own which were in the world, he loved them unto the end. And supper being ended, the devil having now put into the heart of Judas Iscariot, Simon's son, to betray him; Jesus knowing that the Father had given all things into his hands, and that he was come from God, and went to God; He riseth from supper, and laid aside his garments; and took a towel, and girded himself. After that he poureth water into a basin, and began to wash the disciples' feet, and to wipe them with the towel wherewith he was girded. (John 13:1–5)

Let's summarize this remarkable series of events: At the end of the feast of the Passover, Jesus knew that Judas Iscariot—one of His chosen Apostles and closest friends—would betray Him and cause His death. The Lord remarkably washed the feet of the Apostles— even those of Judas, as indicated in verse 11—as a sign of His deep and unfeigned love for them. A lesser leader could not have done that. And one who practiced unrighteous dominion would surely not have demonstrated love for his or her own murderer. At least, he or she would have tried to dissuade him, with force if necessary, from his cruel intention. Many could have justified worse in the name of self-defense.

After Peter objected to what he saw as an inappropriate debasing act for the Son of God, the Lord addressed Peter's concerns about a master washing the feet of His servants. He then revealed Judas's betrayal. But He did it in a way that the Apostles didn't even know whom He was speaking about.

There was obviously no pointing of fingers, no raising of the voice, no completely understandable recriminations or reproaches for this most despicable and cowardly plan: "When Jesus had thus said, he was troubled in spirit, and testified, and said, Verily, verily, I say unto you, that one of you shall betray me. Then the disciples looked one on another, doubting of whom he spake. Now there was leaning on Jesus' bosom one of his disciples, whom Jesus loved. Simon Peter therefore beckoned to him, that he should ask who it should be of whom he spake. He then lying on Jesus' breast saith unto him, Lord, who is it?" (John 13:21–25).

And even when the Lord declared who would betray Him, He did it without any attempt to embarrass Judas or sway him from exercising his agency: "Jesus answered, He it is, to whom I shall give a sop, when I have dipped it. And when he had dipped the sop, he gave it to Judas Iscariot, the son of Simon. And after the sop Satan entered into him. Then said Jesus unto him, That thou doest, do quickly. Now no man at the table knew for what intent he spake this unto him. For some of them thought, because Judas had the bag, that Jesus had said unto him, Buy those things that we have need of against the feast; or, that he should give something to the poor" (John 13:26–29).

Remarkably, the Lord gave them a new commandment. Was the

commandment that Judas should be stopped? That His death should be avenged? No. Though the Savior knew that the betrayal of Judas would cause Him to suffer crucifixion—the most painful and hideous death the Romans could devise as a means of discouraging others from even considering rebellion or breaching the law of their oppressors—the Savior commanded that they each love one another. And He didn't exclude Judas from the list of those who should be loved: "A new commandment I give unto you, That ye love one another; as I have loved you, that ye also love one another. By this shall all men know that ye are my disciples, if ye have love one to another" (John 13:34–35).

The account of this same incident in Matthew is slightly different, adding a brief interaction between the Lord and His betrayer. But even in this account, we read of no angry Lord, no justifiably upset Savior who forced Judas to change his sinful plan to have the Savior tortured and killed for money. All the Lord did was attempt to persuade Judas by quoting a scriptural reference (pure knowledge), likely with far more concern for the soul of His murderer than the prevention of His own excruciating suffering:

> And as they did eat, he said, Verily I say unto you, that one of you shall betray me. And they were exceeding sorrowful, and began every one of them to say unto him, Lord, is it I? And he answered and said, He that dippeth his hand with me in the dish, the same shall betray me. The Son of man goeth as it is written of him: but woe unto that man by whom the Son of man is betrayed! it had been good for that man if he had not been born. Then Judas, which betrayed him, answered and said, Master, is it I? He said unto him, Thou hast said. (Matthew 26:21–25)

Even later, when the actual betrayal occurred, we see no attempt at unrighteous dominion. Remember that the disciples with the Lord had some weapons and were ready to fight to protect themselves. But the Lord commanded them to stand down. I imagine this next scene as something the Lord whispered lovingly to the betrayer: "And while he yet spake, behold a multitude, and he that was called Judas, one of the twelve, went before them, and drew near unto Jesus to kiss him. But Jesus said unto him, Judas, betrayest thou the Son of man with a kiss?" (Luke 22:47–48). This is the only recrimination. What remarkable restraint and unfeigned love.

Summary

A Christlike leader avoids unrighteous dominion of any kind and repents when he or she realizes what is being done. The scriptures and prophets tell us that these unholy practices are widespread, but the Lord requires us to change and follow His example of using the principles of righteousness to lead His Church. The scriptural antidote to unrighteous dominion is to lead "by persuasion, by long-suffering, by gentleness and meekness, and by love unfeigned; by kindness, and pure knowledge, which shall greatly enlarge the soul without hypocrisy, and without guile" (D&C 121:41–42).

In the next chapter, we will review what we can learn from the Savior about how to teach.

Chapter Sixteen: How to Teach

"But, verily I say unto you, teach one another according to the office wherewith I have appointed you" (D&C 38:23)

fter many years training managers how to be more effective leaders, Reenie and I began to better understand the process of teaching. We noticed, for example, that the use of stories and examples improve training. The managers remembered the stories and used them to understand how to apply the instruction to their own situations.

We also found that learner-oriented training far surpassed the effectiveness of trainer-oriented workshops. Trainers, for example, who simply lectured from the trainer manuals we provided them may have covered the required material, but they consistently received much lower scores in teaching effectiveness than those who facilitated active discussions and asked lots of questions to make students think. The use of the case study method and numerous interactive activities made workshops more interesting and valuable, according to student assessments completed after the training. Sessions where managers shared their ideas and best practices with each other were better than those without practical discussions.

And we found that when we applied these same practices in Church leadership assignments—adding the Spirit—we had more success. This shouldn't have surprised us, of course, since the Lord, the master teacher, used these techniques more than two thousand years ago.

Leaders Must Be Teachers

One of the core responsibilities of leaders is teaching. The CHI states,

> All leaders are teachers. . . . Leaders' most powerful teaching comes from their personal example. Leaders also teach by sharing their testimonies and conducting doctrinally based discussions in leadership meetings, classes, and activities. They teach from the scriptures and the words of latter-day prophets. They know that "the preaching of the word . . . [has] more powerful effect . . . than the sword, or anything else" (Alma 31:5). In addition to teaching the gospel themselves, priesthood and auxiliary leaders are responsible for the quality of learning and teaching in their organizations. They ensure that teaching in their classes is meaningful, edifying, and doctrinally sound. (*Handbook 2: Administering the Church*, 2: 3.2.4)

In his powerful book titled *Principles of Priesthood Leadership*, Elder Stephen D. Nadauld of the Seventy said that the *primary* responsibility of priesthood leaders is to teach the plan of redemption (Stephen D. Nadauld, *Principles of Priesthood Leadership* [Salt Lake City: Bookcraft, 1999], 4). The scriptures also reinforce the importance of our teaching role: "And I give unto you a commandment that you shall teach one another the doctrine of the kingdom. Teach ye diligently and my grace shall attend you, that you may be instructed more perfectly in theory, in principle, in doctrine, in the law of the gospel, in all things that pertain unto the kingdom of God, that are expedient for you to understand" (D&C 88:77–78).

The Importance of Teaching Children

This leadership requirement is especially explicit when it comes to children. "And ye will not suffer your children that they go hungry, or naked; neither will ye suffer that they transgress the laws of God, and fight and quarrel one with another, and serve the devil, who is the master of sin, or who is the evil spirit which hath been spoken of by our fathers, he being an enemy to all righteousness. But ye will teach them to walk in the ways of truth and soberness; ye will teach them to love one another, and to serve one another" (Mosiah 4:14–15).

This teaching responsibility of leaders in the home is so essential that we read in Doctrine and Covenants: "And again, inasmuch as parents have children in Zion, or in any of her stakes which are organized, that teach them not to understand the doctrine of repentance, faith in Christ the Son of the living God, and of baptism and the gift of the Holy Ghost by the laying on of the hands, when eight years old, the sin be upon the heads of the parents" (D&C 68:25).

Christlike Teaching

At lds.org, on the "Come, Follow Me: Learning Resources for Youth" page, there is an online guidebook entitled *Teaching the Gospel in the Savior's Way*. At the time of this writing, it suggests the following ten characteristics of the Savior's teaching in the "Teaching in the Savior's Way" section:

- He loved them.
- He knew who they were.
- He prepared Himself.
- He used the scriptures.
- He shared simple stories, parables, and real-life examples.
- He asked questions.
- He invited them to testify.
- He trusted them.
- He invited them to act in faith.
- He was their example and mentor.

Then it says, "This . . . is your sacred calling—to teach as the Savior taught. As you do, the youth will give place in their hearts for the seed of the gospel to be planted, to swell, and to grow. This will lead to conversion—the ultimate goal of your teaching. As you help youth become converted, you help them prepare to follow the Savior throughout their lives—to worthily attend the temple, receive the Melchizedek Priesthood, serve missions, make sacred covenants, raise righteous families, and build God's kingdom in all the world. How great will be your joy!" (*Teaching the Gospel in the Savior's Way*, "Come, Follow Me: Learning Resources for Youth," http://www.lds.org).

The same could be said, of course, of teaching adults.

How the Lord Taught

Let's examine in more detail some of the teaching methods the Lord used that caused reactions like this: "And when he was come into his own country, he taught them in their synagogue, insomuch that they were astonished, and said, Whence hath this man this wisdom, and these mighty works?" (Matthew 13:54). Specifically, let's review the use of parables, scriptures, questions, invitations to act, and teaching by the Spirit.

Parables

In Mark, we read, "And he taught them many things by parables" (Mark 4:2). Matthew added, "All these things spake Jesus unto the multitude in parables; and without a parable spake he not unto them: That it might be fulfilled which was spoken by the prophet, saying, I will open my mouth in parables; I will utter things which have been kept secret from the foundation of the world" (Matthew 13:34–35).

We know that there are several reasons the Lord used this technique of telling a story to illustrate a gospel principle. The curious disciples inquired: "Why speakest thou unto them in parables? He answered and said unto them, Because it is given unto you to know the mysteries of the kingdom of heaven, but to them it is not given. For whosoever hath, to him shall be given, and he shall have more abundance: but whosoever hath not, from him shall be taken away even that he hath. Therefore speak I to them in parables: because they seeing see not; and hearing they hear not, neither do they understand" (Matthew 13:10–13).

Thus, one reason the Lord used parables is to allow the believers to understand the deeper truth embedded in the teaching while the unbelievers would simply be entertained. Everybody likes a good story. But the Lord acknowledged that this reason was only temporary: "These things have I spoken unto you in proverbs: but the time cometh, when I shall no more speak unto you in proverbs, but I shall shew you plainly of the Father" (John 16:25).

So why else would he use stories? The genius of parables is multi-dimensional. For example, one of my professors in graduate school, Alan Wilkins, researched the topic of how storytelling affects corporate culture for his doctoral thesis at Stanford University (see Alan L. Wilkins, *Developing Corporate Character* [San Francisco: Jossey-Bass, 1989], 101–2). His work indicated that stories are the most powerful way of teaching organizational values. Why? Because they help explain complex and important concepts. People can relate them by memory. They spread widely and quickly throughout the organization. Think about it. Could you, without looking, write down the Ten Commandments in order? Most people only remember the first few correctly because our minds aren't good at remembering lists, even important ones. But I bet you know the parable of the Good Samaritan. Even Primary children can tell that story from heart.

Parables encapsulate and convey doctrine in a way that helps people understand what otherwise might just be abstract notion. They touch people. They help us understand how the commandments apply in real life. They bring gospel principles alive. The stories are transportable and can easily be shared with others.

Listen to general conference carefully to see how they work. Rare is the talk that doesn't include a story. I'm can remember several of them from memory that I've used in teaching moments over the years. President Boyd K. Packer, for example, was a master teacher. I can't tell you how many times I've used his stories about how sin is like a crocodile patiently waiting for us to approach. Or how describing the Spirit is like describing salt to someone who has never tasted it. Or how bad thoughts can be pushed off of the stage of our mind with something like a hymn. (Along with *Teaching No Greater Call*, there simply isn't a better book on teaching the gospel than President Packer's classic, *Teach Ye Diligently*.)

Using these parables teaches gospel truths so much more effectively than simply lecturing about the importance of avoiding sins, the difficulty of explaining how the Spirit feels, or how we need to change our impure thoughts.

Different Types of Parables

Stories, proverbs, comparisons (such as similes and metaphors), and examples are all different types of parables. The Lord used them all. We've already discussed stories, but consider this skillful example of using similes to illustrate and clarify gospel concepts: "Then said he,

Unto what is the kingdom of God like? and whereunto shall I resemble it? It is like a grain of mustard seed, which a man took, and cast into his garden; and it grew, and waxed a great tree; and the fowls of the air lodged in the branches of it. And again he said, Whereunto shall I liken the kingdom of God? It is like leaven, which a woman took and hid in three measures of meal, till the whole was leavened" (Luke 13:18–21).

Here is an example of a metaphor on the same topic (the kingdom of God): "And the scribes which came down from Jerusalem said, He hath Beelzebub, and by the prince of the devils casteth he out devils. And he called them unto him, and said unto them in parables, How can Satan cast out Satan? And if a kingdom be divided against itself, that kingdom cannot stand. And if a house be divided against itself, that house cannot stand" (Mark 3:22–25).

The Lord also used examples. For instance, when He taught the Apostles how to pray, He certainly wasn't instructing them to use only the prayer we now refer to as the Lord's Prayer (Matthew 6:10–13). But as the master teacher, He wanted to give them a specific example of what a prayer might look like, in the same way a modern-day teacher might help young men or women use roleplays to learn the specific types of words they could use to decline a friend's invitation to sin.

Scriptures

We have already discussed at length how the Lord (as a gospel scholar) used scripture, but I include a short reminder to use the scriptures in this chapter to reinforce, again, the power of the canonized written word. If the Lord, who is the author of scripture, exemplifies the need of referring to them, we can do nothing less. I try to follow the guideline I heard from a returned missionary, who had been instructed by his mission president that even in a short talk from the pulpit no fewer than two scriptures should be used to teach any gospel principle. If the minimum of two scriptures can't be found, we should reconsider the topic.

Questions

In His teaching, the Lord would often follow a parable with a question. Why did He do that? (Notice that when I ask you a question that you stop to think, become more engaged, and pay more attention than when I don't.) Asking questions involves the listeners. It doesn't allow for daydreaming or being passive. It motivates them to learn.

For example, to answer the question that a lawyer asked of Him, the Lord relayed the parable of the good Samaritan. After the story, He asked the question, "Which now of these three, thinkest thou, was neighbour unto him that fell among the thieves?" The lawyer then answered, "He that shewed mercy on him. Then said Jesus unto him, Go, and do thou likewise" (Luke 10:36–37).

Why did the Master ask him a question? Because once the student answered the question, the student knew the lesson of the good Samaritan. The Lord didn't need to repeat it because the lawyer had already taught himself. And as you know, the lessons we teach ourselves are much more likely to be remembered and acted upon than those taught to us by another.

Note how the Lord used questions to engage the learner in one more example: "And, behold, a certain lawyer stood up, and tempted him, saying, Master, what shall I do to inherit eternal life? He said unto him, What is written in the law? how readest thou? And he answering said, Thou shalt love the Lord thy God with all thy heart, and with all thy soul, and with all thy strength, and with all thy mind; and thy neighbour as thyself. And he said unto him, Thou hast answered right: this do, and thou shalt live" (Luke 10:25–28).

By asking skillful questions in each of these teaching moments, the Lord led the engaged learner to powerful and memorable insights without lecturing.

Invitations to Act

At the end of the lesson with the second lawyer, note how the Savior said, "This do and thou shalt live." That was an invitation to not only hear the word but to do the word. Similarly, the parable of the good Samaritan illustrates how the Lord invited people to take action on gospel teachings. Thus, he said, "Go, and do thou likewise" to the first lawyer. And he instructed the woman who was to be stoned for adultery to "go and sin no more," and the Apostles to whom He would teach the Lord's prayer to "after this manner therefore pray thee" (Matthew 6:9).

This occurs so often in the teachings of the Lord that I believe a pattern can be suggested. Generally speaking, the teaching method of the

Lord concluded with a call to action. We can emulate His example by asking "will you" questions such as, "Will you apply this principle this week?" Or, "Will you accept the assignment of _____?"

Teaching by the Spirit

In Mark, we read, "And they went into Capernaum; and straightway on the sabbath day he entered into the synagogue, and taught. And they were astonished at his doctrine: for he taught them as one that had authority, and not as the scribes" (Mark 1:21–22).

The Lord has provided a way for us to teach with similar authority to Him. But it is conditional on our use of the power of the Spirit. Luke explained, "For the Holy Ghost shall teach you in the same hour what ye ought to say" (Luke 12:12). Further light and knowledge on the subject is revealed in the Doctrine and Covenants: "Seek not to declare my word, but first seek to obtain my word, and then shall your tongue be loosed; then, if you desire, you shall have my Spirit and my word, yea, the power of God unto the convincing of men" (D&C 11:21).

Consider this sobering reminder: "And the Spirit shall be given unto you by the prayer of faith; and if ye receive not the Spirit ye shall not teach" (D&C 42:14).

A powerful way to bring the confirmation of the Spirit into teaching is to include our testimonies. If we have explained the doctrine correctly, the Spirit will manifest the truthfulness of it to the learner as we testify. Another important way of using the Spirit is to pray during preparation time to be guided, and then again at the beginning of the teaching opportunity to be directed by the Spirit. As my wife has often taught, "It is better to use your time praying about what to teach than using it to create amazing handouts." Even the cleverest of us needs to avoid the temptation of relying on the arm of flesh.

All of these teaching techniques can be summarized in Figure 16-1.

Figure 16-1: Christlike Teaching

Technique	Description	Examples
Parables	Using stories, proverbs, comparisons, and examples to clarify gospel principles and make them memorable	• Let me give you an example. • Here is a story that illustrates the principle. • I have asked Brother Johnson to share a personal experience.
Scriptures	Using the canonized word of God to ground teaching in accurate doctrine and reinforce the importance of personal gospel study	• Let's read together what the Savior said. • Who can find a scripture to support what we have been discussing? • Sister Ramos, would you read the scripture we just mentioned?
Questions	Engaging learners in the process of learning by creating high degrees of interaction	• How does this gospel principle apply to your life? • Who has had an experience with this that they would be willing to share with us? • What would you do in the situation I just described? • How will you avoid the problems we just discussed?

Invitations to act	Extending invitations to learners to take action and apply gospel principles in their lives	• Who is available to help us next week? • Will you accept the assignment? • What is your plan to apply the principles we discussed? • So will you try _____ when you go home today?
Teaching by the Spirit	Preparing sufficiently to be directed by the Spirit and being sensitive to promptings during teaching	• Allow me to share a scripture that comes to mind. • I feel impressed to tell you about an experience I had. • I would like to bear my testimony . . .

Summary

The Savior was the best teacher in history. By using the methods He employed, we can improve the effectiveness of our teaching and become more Christlike leaders. Specifically, by using parables—whether they are stories, proverbs, similes, metaphors, or examples—we can better clarify gospel topics. We also need to, as He did, use the scriptures. Following parable and scripture-based instruction with questions to engage learners and drive home the learning is a powerful technique. Also, extending an invitation to take action improves the probability that those we teach will be "doers of the word, and not hearers only" (James 1:22). In addition, the scriptures instruct us that we should never teach without the Spirit. This requires preparation and humility.

In the next chapter, we will discuss another difficult leadership skill: correcting others.

Chapter Seventeen: How to Correct Others

"Reproving betimes with sharpness, when moved upon by the Holy Ghost; and then showing forth afterwards an increase of love toward him whom thou hast reproved, lest he esteem thee to be his enemy" (D&C 121:43)

*O*ne of the most difficult tasks of leadership is the correction of others. I still remember the discomfort I felt as a new elders quorum president when the bishop instructed me to sit down with a few of the home teachers over whom I had stewardship and call them to repentance for not doing the work they had been assigned. Each of them was older than I was, and I felt odd correcting them.

I don't think I'm alone in this feeling. I remember my father telling me the story of how he once had to correct false doctrine from the pulpit when he served in a bishopric. He had great anxiety about how to do it until he received an answer to his silent prayers about what he should say. He stood up and clarified the doctrine using the words that had been given him in a way that minimized embarrassment to the speaker. What did he say? It was something like, "We want to thank our speaker for sharing his opinion with us today. President Kimball has suggested another way to look at this same issue. In the last general conference, he said . . ."

Part of the reason so many of us are reluctant to correct others in the Church is that we are concerned about hurting feelings or causing offense. But when done properly, correction can—and should—actually be a demonstration of love. This is what the Lord explained in D&C 95, when He said, "Verily, thus saith the Lord unto you whom I love, and whom I love I also chasten that their sins may be forgiven, for with the chastisement I prepare a way for their deliverance in all things out of temptation, and I have loved you" (D&C 95:1).

As leaders, this is a good place to start. When we correct others, it must be done in a spirit of love, not to punish or chastise. And as Moroni instructed, "Wherefore, my beloved brethren, pray unto the Father with all the energy of heart, that ye may be filled with this love" (Moroni 7:48).

How Did the Lord Correct Others?

President Spencer W. Kimball illustrated how the Lord corrected others: "Jesus was a patient, pleading, loving leader. When Peter drew his sword and smote the high priest's servant, cutting off his right ear, Jesus said, 'Put up thy sword into the sheath' (John 18:11). Without being angry or perturbed, Jesus quietly healed the servant's ear (see Luke 22:51). His reproof of Peter was kind, yet firm. Because Jesus loved his followers, he was able to level with them, to be candid and forthright with them. He reproved Peter at times because he loved him, and Peter, being a great man, was able to grow from this reproof" ("Jesus: The Perfect Leader").

We learn in Proverbs: "The ear that heareth the reproof of life abideth among the wise. He that refuseth instruction despiseth his own soul: but he that heareth reproof getteth understanding" (Proverbs 15:31–32).

Consider another example from the life of the Savior we referenced earlier. Let's examine the gentle, firm, but loving reproof offered both to the accusers and the accused in the story of the adulterous woman: "When Jesus had lifted up himself, and saw none but the woman, he said unto her, Woman, where are those thine accusers? hath no man condemned thee? She said, No man, Lord. And Jesus said unto her, Neither do I condemn thee: go, and sin no more" (John 8:3-11).

We see no recrimination or disrespectful language. There is no evidence of anger. No loss of emotional control. No sarcasm, no chastisement. To the accusers He simply asked them to evaluate their own potential hypocrisy. And, as the scriptures report, they left "being convicted by their own conscience." To the accused, He offered calm and loving instruction rather than condemnation. While this example is instructive for any Church leader, it is especially helpful for leaders of homes who understand that exhaustion, impatience, and established patterns of behavior can easily interfere with our ability to correct with love. In the home especially, leaders can't allow even stressful corrective situations to devolve into venues for potential abuse or unrighteous dominion.

The Scriptural Instruction for Reproving Others

So how do we correct others properly? Let's examine the instruction offered in the scripture that opened this chapter. D&C 121:43 can be broken into four parts: "reproving betimes," "with sharpness," "when moved upon by the Holy Ghost," "and then showing forth afterwards an increase of love." We'll consider each part separately.

Reprove Betimes

Part one of the scriptural admonition suggests that reproof is a choice. Not every incorrect action displayed by those over whom we have stewardship requires leadership reproof. Decide whether to intervene by considering the following types of questions:

- What are the probable consequences of not correcting this action (or mistake or oversight)?
- Will it cause important damage to anyone or to the good name of the Church?
- Does the importance of the correction outweigh the risk of embarrassment or offense?
- Do I have the information necessary to interject myself into this situation, or do I only know part of the story? What do I need to know before I can decide whether to offer reproof or not?
- Am I the right person to offer correction, or should it be someone else?

- Am I sure the situation needs correction, or was someone just doing something differently than I would do it?
- Do I know how to correct the situation, or should I get some advice from my priesthood leader first? Do I know how to offer loving feedback? If not, is there someone who can help me learn to do it skillfully?
- Is the reason I want to offer correction my honest concern for the welfare of the person, or is it because I want to get something off my chest?
- Do I have control of my emotions, or will anger, apathy, or resentment make it difficult for me to offer constructive criticism?

The dictionary definition of *betimes* suggests timeliness. If reproofs are appropriate, they should be delivered as quickly as possible. This is important for both the giver and the receiver of correction. For the receiver, timeliness increases the likelihood that the mistake will be corrected because it is still "fresh." The receiver will likely remember what he or she did, why he or she did it, and avoid repeating the mistake and making it habitual. For the giver, timely reproof reduces the likelihood that a delay will allow anger, distrust, or resentment to build before a discussion can occur.

With Sharpness

Sharpness in this scripture, of course, means precision or focus—not anger. A correction is not useful if the person doesn't understand precisely what was wrong and exactly how to correct it. For example, saying, "Brother Witcomb, you need to be a better home teacher" is not helpful. Saying, "Brother Witcomb, next month, could you find out what we need to do to help the Monsons with Kaley's illness?" is more clear. In the former example, the person only feels judged and chastised. In the latter, the person understands how to improve. See Figure 17-1 for more examples of how to sharpen the focus of constructive criticism.

Figure 17-1: Examples of Unfocused versus Sharp Reproofs

Unfocused	Sharp
• Please be more organized about quorum assignments in your calling as our secretary. • Don't teach false doctrine. • I know you're really trying to work hard and do a good job with your calling, but sometimes what you say isn't quite right, and it tends to offend some of the more sensitive and newer members of the Church who might not realize what a wonderful and well-intended person you are. • Girls, you need to be more inclusive and welcoming to everyone. • You need to keep the commandments. You make lots of people uncomfortable. Several of them have talked to me about the way you speak with your kids.	• Please call or text people to remind them one week before their assignments. • When you told people last week that the Word of Wisdom is optional, that wasn't actually correct. I have written down some references to the doctrine here. • Sister Mabel told me she felt offended when you said that new members usually aren't fully converted. Would you mind very much talking to her and apologizing? • Young women, please don't sit with the same people every week. And please introduce yourself to any visitors. • Brother Mann, I heard you raise your voice with your kids in church this morning. As your bishop, I think it would be a good idea if you came in to talk with me this afternoon at two. I think I can help.

As the figure suggests, specific examples are required when giving constructive criticism so that people understand both what was incorrect and how to improve. General, unfocused observations or expectations are insufficient and inconsistent with this scriptural admonition.

When Moved upon by the Holy Ghost

Elder Spencer J. Condie suggested several conditions for determining whether the Holy Ghost has guided a reproof or not. One is whether "the intensity of the reproof is appropriate to the cause," and he gives the example of Joseph Smith rebuking the guards in the Liberty Jail and the Savior expelling the moneychangers from the temple as examples of intense and unusual reproofs. But that level of response would be inappropriate for all but a few extraordinary situations. He also suggested, "We weigh our words—and our feelings—carefully. . . . We don't seek to harm, to stretch the truth, or to overstate the problem. Our objective is to sincerely help the other person and address the specific issue at hand. We don't make him feel inferior."

He then shared this interesting personal experience:

> On one occasion I was called to counsel with a family in trouble. The father had inflicted physical punishment on his wife and children. Several hours before we met together, I thought about what I should tell them. I fully intended to begin my remarks to this unkind husband with the spirit of "Ye fiend of the eternal pit"; but the night I met them, I heard myself saying, "Fred, I love you, and I love your wife and family. I'd like to help you build an eternal home." He was no longer defensive. His wife was no longer interested in finding fault. They were anxious to make new commitments and forget an unpleasant past history. They were teachable and amenable to some very pointed counsel. ("Reproving with Love," *Ensign*, August 1979)

When we give reproofs as moved upon by the Holy Ghost, there is always a spirit of love, which leads us to the final step in the process of correcting others.

Show Forth Afterward an Increase of Love

Brigham Young gave us a key to righteous reproving: "If you are ever called to chasten a person, never chasten beyond the balm you have within you to bind up. . . . When you have the chastening rod in your hands, ask God to give you wisdom to use it, that you may not use it to the destruction of an individual, but to his salvation" ("Varieties of Mind, Etc.," *Journal of Discourses*, Vol. 9, [London: Latter-day Saints' Book Depot, 1862] 9:124–25).

After the discussion, the Christlike leader always offers whatever assistance is necessary to help the individual make the correction. This is a powerful manifestation of love. I also think it is usually a good idea to quickly review the necessary corrections and ensure clarity by asking for questions. Another powerful manifestation of love is then to express confidence that, with the help of the Lord, the individual can make any necessary changes. We are all imperfect, and without these reproofs from others who love us, none of us would be able to return to our Father in Heaven.

I believe it is a good practice to emphasize these truths in a prayer that closes the discussion. I have often prayed something like this: "Father in Heaven, I am so grateful for [name]. He is a wonderful man and I am thankful to work with him. Please help him do what he feels he needs to do to draw closer to thee. And help me support him in his efforts. We are grateful for the Savior's Atonement and pray that thou will forgive us both of our sins and shortcomings as we strive to be more faithful servants."

Respect Privacy and Confidences

The scriptures also suggest other considerations about these discussions. For example, we learn in D&C 42 that sensitive discussions such as these should be conducted privately, not publicly: "Thou shalt take him or her between him or her and thee alone; and if he or she confess thou shalt be reconciled. And if he or she confess not thou shalt deliver him or her up unto the church, not to the members, but to the elders. And it shall be done in a meeting, and that not before the world" (D&C 42:88–89).

In an article in the *Ensign*, marriage and family therapist Randy Keyes added, "Unless the whole ward is in need of a reprimand, it is better for a bishop to speak to the individual rather than to use the collective approach. Similarly, a child or spouse has the right to be told privately of mistakes. Public correction is often cruel or, at the least, misguided" ("Counseling together in Marriage," *Ensign*, June 2012).

A Word about Disciplinary Councils

When mistakes and oversight rise to the level of serious sin, leaders should urge those they love to participate in the cleansing power of the Atonement. For most of our sins, the repentance process doesn't need to involve anyone beyond the individual, the Lord, and those who have been harmed. But for certain serious sins, a confession to the bishop is warranted.

In addition to counseling sessions and other supports and resources, the bishop may need to utilize a ward disciplinary council, or refer the person to a stake disciplinary council in some cases. A detailed description of this process falls beyond the scope of this book because so few Church leaders normally participate in this sweet cleansing process.

But I will tell you from many years of personal involvement in these sacred meetings that they are some of the most spiritual, uplifting, supportive, and loving councils of the Church. There is something special about meetings that are focused entirely on the application of the atoning power of Jesus Christ. For those who may have the opportunity to participate in these sacred councils, I urge you to carefully read everything about them contained in the CHI for more information about how to conduct or participate in them correctly.

Summary

Though correcting others can be a difficult part of Church leadership, it is an important skill for the Christlike leader, who loves people enough to want to help them improve their lives and service. The Lord has given us several examples of how to correct others properly, demonstrating both the compassion and the gentle firmness required. And following the admonition in D&C 121:43 to "reproving betimes," "with sharpness," "when moved upon by the Holy Ghost," "and then showing forth afterwards an increase of love" will help the Christlike leader reprove appropriately while minimizing the potential unintended consequences of giving offense.

In the final chapter, let's review the competencies of Christlike leadership and discuss what may be the most important quality of those who strive to follow the Lord's example: shepherding.

CHAPTER EIGHTEEN: HOW TO SHEPHERD

"Inasmuch as ye have done it unto one of the least of these my brethren, ye have done it unto me" (Matthew 25:40)

*T*he leadership ministry of the Lord is remarkable for many reasons. One reason is the incredible breadth of His skills, which ranged from the intense emotional and physical power of righteous indignation required of Him to cleanse the temple to the sensitive tenderness necessary for healing a sick child or raising the dead. He could confound the best educated and most powerful Pharisees and Sadducees with stories or teach with such powerful simplicity that the weak and unschooled could understand complex gospel truth. He lifted the weary and comforted the downtrodden. He calmed the bloodlust in a mob with a whispered question. He healed those that raised weapons against Him. He converted His enemies. He both loved and chastened His friends.

He is also remarkable because, unlike His historical counterparts, He was consistent and without error. We see no leadership mistakes, lapses of judgment, selfish inclinations, cowardliness, exploitation of others, awkward missteps, or corruption through absolute power. Unlike our much celebrated leadership heroes of the past who often displayed extraordinary competence in some things, He displayed it in *all* things.

And though we can't duplicate His perfection in this regard, there is not a single one among us who can't improve our leadership effectiveness by emulating His example, thereby doing what He commanded when He pled with us to "come, follow me."

A Summary of the Lord's Attributes and Leadership Competencies

He displayed virtue, temperance, godliness, knowledge, faith, hope, humility, obedience, diligence, courage, patience, charity, and brotherly kindness. And in this book, I have tried to illustrate His leadership abilities in several key areas, including the seven competencies listed in the model below (see Figure 18-1). The Savior is an exemplar, scholar, believer, seeker, disciple, teacher, and shepherd, aspects of which we can and should incorporate into our own leadership practices.

Figure 18-1: The Christlike Leader

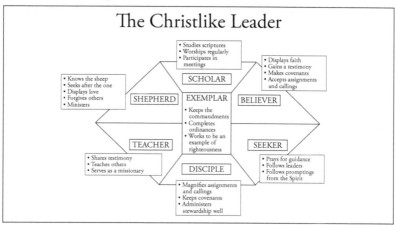

In this closing chapter, we will discuss what many believe to be His most powerful leadership competency: shepherding. Following the pattern established by the Lord, let's open the discussion of shepherding with a story.

Sheepherding and Shepherding

When I was in high school, my parents sold our home in Salt Lake and bought a historical old farmhouse in Draper, Utah, when the town was still what would be considered a rural community. On the farm stood chicken coops and a large barn, and it had plenty of room to keep horses, grow a large garden, and store my father's burgeoning collection of classic automobiles that would be restored.

When we moved into the house, my parents negotiated with the previous owners to keep some of the artifacts from the home's original owner, J. R. Allen. I still chuckle when thinking about some of the framed sheep photos that hung in the house when I was a teenager. They sported a turn of the nineteenth–century formality, with long-haired sheep looking as though they were posing for the photographer.

Brother Allen had been a sheep-man and was quite famous for his prize-winning animals, including his sheepdogs, which had apparently been recognized for their superb prowess. They served as sheepherders, often without human supervision. I heard some of the old-timers in town speak in almost reverent tones of the way the well-trained Allen dogs of long ago could form the sheep into tightly bundled groups and drive them safely to any intended destination. The dogs could bark and heel-nip the sheep into submission, protecting them from coyotes and cougars during their long grazing drives to and from nearby hills.

The summer after our move, I participated as one of three LDS Scouts in a special friendship tour organized by the BSA. Our group of mostly Jewish Boy Scouts represented troops from across the nation, who traveled as US ambassadors to Israel. During our six-week trip, we camped with Israeli Scouts and toured the Holy Land, roaming around the brown, rolling hills of the country in a lumbering bus.

At one point in the tour, I noticed a group of sheep and was surprised to see them attended by a long-robed shepherd carrying the same sort of curled wooden crook I had seen in New Testament paintings. As I watched, the shepherd turned his back to the sheep and appeared to leave them. Based on what I thought I knew about sheep, I assumed he had recklessly abandoned his responsibility. He casually strode off down the road, alone.

But then something interesting happened. Slowly, the sheep lifted their heads from grazing, noted the shepherd's absence, and followed after him, quickly closing the gap between them and their leader.

I had believed that without the aid of dogs, the shepherd would have to shout or wave his crook to get the sheep's attention, finding a way to push them ahead of him down the dusty road if he wanted them to move. He proved me wrong. There was no barking or heel-nipping involved. The shepherd led from the front instead of pushing the sheep ahead of him.

This experience has served as metaphor for our firm—a sort of parable if you will—about the difference between good leaders and great ones. Reenie and I often use it in our leadership training to show that it takes a lot of patience, trust, and courage to be a shepherd (Kimball Fisher, *Leading Self-Directed Work Teams* [New York: McGraw-Hill, Revised edition, 2000], 117–19).

The approaches of the two leaders are different. The sheepherder uses coercion, pushing, and force. He or she has good intentions and often successfully protects his or her charges from outside threats. But the sheepherder leads from behind (without setting a visible example of how the sheep can move themselves), seldom trusts that the flock will move without his or her prodding, and uses methods that create dependence on the leader—not self-reliance.

Alternatively, the shepherd respects agency and teaches his or her charges to be self-reliant. Had the sheep in the example above not been lovingly taught and cared for, they probably would have scattered, as I feared they would. But when properly taught and trusted, the charges of a good shepherd choose to follow him or her willingly. See Figure 18-2 for a summary of differences.

Figure 18-2: Sheepherders versus Shepherds

	Sheepherders	Shepherds
Illustrative methods	Barking, heel-nipping, pushing, prodding, ordering, forcing, and so on	Teaching, training, trusting, caring, loving, offering choices, and so on

Positions relative to the flock	Behind. (Believes the sheep need to be pushed. Worries that agency is risky. Thinks you can't keep your eyes on the sheep unless you are behind them. Believes it is more important to focus on avoiding past problems than looking to the future.)	In front. (Trusts that if the sheep are properly taught that they will choose to follow the right. Respects agency. Thinks you can't keep your eyes on the road ahead unless you are in front. Sees the need of leading out and setting an example.)
Outcomes	Creates leader-reliance	Creates self-reliance

The Hireling versus the Shepherd

The Lord further refined this point in the parable of the hireling versus the shepherd. In John 10, we read, "I am the good shepherd: the good shepherd giveth his life for the sheep. But he that is an hireling, and not the shepherd, whose own the sheep are not, seeth the wolf coming, and leaveth the sheep, and fleeth: and the wolf catcheth them, and scattereth the sheep. The hireling fleeth, because he is an hireling, and careth not for the sheep. I am the good shepherd, and know my sheep, and am known of mine. As the Father knoweth me, even so know I the Father: and I lay down my life for the sheep" (John 10:11–15).

Several points from this scripture deserve elaboration. First, the Lord noted that He, as the good shepherd, is willing to give His life for us. Without His atoning sacrifice, we cannot be saved from that great wolf Satan, who would otherwise scatter the flock.

Second, someone who treats a Church calling like a job is never willing to do what is necessary for the sheep. A hireling who is motivated by money (or, for that matter, by prestige, guilt, peer pressure, or anything other than genuine caring for those within his or her stewardship) will run away at the first sign of danger (or difficulty, inconvenience, or whenever something more interesting comes along).

Third, a good shepherd both knows the sheep and is known by them. This can only occur through an investment of time in personal ministry. Can you really know someone who is a casual acquaintance you only see on Sunday? Can they really know you?

Fourth, a good shepherd knows and is known by God. This relationship also takes a committed investment of time in gospel study, meditation, and prayer. Similarly, it is one thing to say that you know *about* Jesus Christ and another thing entirely to say that you know Jesus Christ. That comes only from a different level of study, obedience, and discipleship.

How the Lord Shepherded

Let's look at an example of how the Lord shepherded, and how that can inform our own leadership practices.

My favorite chapter of scripture is 3 Nephi 17, where the Savior ministered to the Nephites. After He finished teaching them, He did something extraordinary. Let's consider the story in some detail, starting with the fifth verse: "And it came to pass that when Jesus had thus spoken, he cast his eyes round about again on the multitude, and beheld they were in tears, and did look steadfastly upon him as if they would ask him to tarry a little longer with them" (3 Nephi 17:5).

Once His teaching assignment was completed, the Lord tarried. Surely His commitments as the only begotten Son of God were burdensome. Would anyone have more to do, or have a tighter schedule, than Him? We learn in verse four, for example, that He imminently needed to return to His Father and also show Himself to the lost tribes of Israel. After His exhausting assignment, He must have had personal needs for rest and nourishment as well. And yet, He tarried. Why? And for that matter, why did He feed the five thousand? Why did He heal the lame, speak to the adulteress and the Samaritan at the well, or heal the nine ungrateful lepers? The answer is in the next verse.

"And he said unto them: Behold, my bowels are filled with compassion towards you" (3 Nephi 17:6). The Savior was motivated by compassion. We sometimes call it charity, or the true love of Christ—a love so full and Christlike that we give it a special name. It was such a powerful force within the Lord that He described it as a physiological phenomenon. But unlike many of us, He didn't stop here and say, "I love you. It's been wonderful meeting with you. I'm so sorry that I have to go." He allowed His compassion to motivate Him to further action.

In the next verse, we read, "Have ye any that are sick among you? Bring them hither. Have ye any that are lame, or blind, or halt, or maimed, or leprous, or that are withered, or that are deaf, or that are afflicted in any manner? Bring them hither and I will heal them, for I have compassion upon you; my bowels are filled with mercy" (3 Nephi 17:7). The good shepherd didn't ask for a rest or drink of water; He didn't say, "Let me take care of a few things and get back to you tomorrow." He wanted to serve.

Now, remember that He had been teaching since chapter 11. In verse three, He had already ended this conference and asked people to go home and ponder His words overnight until their meeting on the following day. It is probably late. But the Shepherd needs to minister because that was what the sheep needed from Him. And it was not only the sick and afflicted who benefited. He wanted everyone to witness the healings, and He knew they had sufficient faith for a miracle: "For I perceive that ye desire that I should show unto you what I have done unto your brethren at Jerusalem, for I see that your faith is sufficient that I should heal you" (3 Nephi 17:8).

So "it came to pass that when he had thus spoken, all the multitude, with one accord, did go forth with their sick and their afflicted, and their lame, and with their blind, and with their dumb, and with all them that were afflicted in any manner; and he did heal them every one as they were brought forth unto him. And they did all, both they who had been healed and they who were whole, bow down at his feet, and did worship him; and as many as could come for the multitude did kiss his feet, insomuch that they did bathe his feet with their tears" (3 Nephi 17:9–10).

How many came forward? A few dozen? A hundred? Several hundred? More? We don't know. The scriptures only define the crowd He was addressing as "a multitude." This is the term used to describe a great number, such as the group that was so big that the Lord had to enter into a ship to preach to them as they lined the seashore (Mark 4:1), or to describe the host of Midianites and Amalekites who filled a valley and whose camels were "without number" as "the sand by the sea side" (Judges 7:12). *Multitude* was also the word used to describe the five thousand men (plus their wives and children) whom Jesus fed with the five loaves and two fishes (Matthew 14:19).

But despite their large number, the good Shepherd healed "them every one" individually. This one-on-one ministry is what characterizes shepherding.

Then comes the most tender scriptures for me:

> And it came to pass that he commanded that their little children should be brought. So they brought their little children and set them down upon the ground round about him, and Jesus stood in the midst; and the multitude gave way till they had all been brought unto him . . . and he took their little children, *one by one*, and blessed them, and prayed unto the Father for them. And when he had done this he wept again; and he spake unto the multitude, and said unto them: Behold your little ones. And as they looked to behold they cast their eyes towards heaven, and they saw the heavens open, and they saw angels descending out of heaven as it were in the midst of fire; and they came down and encircled those little ones about, and they were encircled about with fire; and the angels did minister unto them. (3 Nephi 17:11–12, 21–24; emphasis added)

I don't remember the last time I read these verses with dry eyes. Is it possible to view them without feeling the Savior's outpouring of love? This, I believe, is the essence of shepherding—that distinctive pure love of Christ. Can you imagine Him blessing every single child of the multitude, giving every single child a few precious personal moments? No wonder there was two hundred years of peace following the Savior's ministry to the Nephites. Those children who were old enough to remember undoubtedly told their children and grandchildren and great-grandchildren what it felt like to receive a personal blessing at the hand of the good Shepherd. I'll bet those great-grandchildren told the stories to their own great-grandchildren as well.

As this wonderful example of the Lord's ministry indicates, shepherding isn't done in large groups during worship services or administrative meetings. It is done one-on-one, as needed, wherever the sheep are found.

I witnessed a powerful example of shepherding while I was writing this book. Bishop Dean M. Davies, who then served as the second counselor in the Presiding Bishopric of the Church, visited our ward. He spoke in sacrament meeting, high priests group meeting, and ward council, with each address being articulate, Spirit-filled, and uplifting. But I believe the most powerful contribution I saw him make that day happened behind the closed doors of a classroom when he responded to a prompting and offered to give a blessing to a mother in our ward who was battling cancer. Assisted by her husband and myself, this Christlike leader, who had only moments before found out about this sister's condition, laid his hands on her head and—following the pattern established by the Lord—gave her a sweet and powerful blessing that brought much-needed comfort. I was touched by his words during the public and leadership meetings. But it was his personal ministry to one family in need that I will never forget.

Bless the Needy

In Alma 34, after preaching about the importance of personal religious devotion, Almulek said, "After ye have done all these things, if ye turn away the needy, and the naked, and visit not the sick and the afflicted, and impart of your substance, if ye have, to those . . . in need—I say unto you, if ye do not any of these things, behold, your prayer is vain, and availeth you nothing, and ye are as the hypocrites who do deny the faith" (Alma 34:28). Similarly, we read in Mormon, "Why do ye adorn yourselves with that which hath no life, and yet suffer the hungry, and the needy, and the naked, and the sick and the afflicted to pass by you, and notice them not" (Mormon 8:39).

It is our responsibility as shepherds to minister to those in spiritual or temporal need. It is both the most difficult and the most joyful of the leadership competencies. We are blessed to witness the examples of leaders such as President Thomas S. Monson, whose shepherding ministry as a young bishop, for example, included caring for eighty-five widows in the 67th Ward in Salt Lake City. He visited these sisters regularly, even after he was released as bishop.

I, of course, do not believe that the Lord expects us to eliminate loneliness, poverty, and disease through our shepherding ministry. Even He acknowledged that the poor will always be with us (Matthew 26:11;

John 12:8; Mark 14:7). But I do believe that we should follow His example as the good Shepherd to bless those in need who are within our stewardship if we want to be a Christlike leader.

The Church has provided wise counsel on the ways to do this so as not to create dependence on the dole or to diminish the self-worth of the individual, and it is a wise leader who understands and applies these inspired methods, as outlined in the CHI. Remember that we cannot do everything—but we can do something, and that we should "be not weary in well-doing, for ye are laying the foundation of a great work. And out of small things proceedeth that which is great" (D&C 64:33).

A Note on Enduring to the End

In this final chapter, it is probably appropriate to mention the importance of endurance. The work of the Christlike leader is great and can be taxing, but there are wonderful blessings for those who carry on: "And, if you keep my commandments and endure to the end you shall have eternal life, which gift is the greatest of all the gifts of God" (D&C 14:7). President Russell M. Nelson reminded us,

> A[n] . . . aspect of the Lord's ministry is His commitment to endure to the end. Never did He withdraw from His assignment. Though He experienced suffering beyond our comprehension, He was not a quitter. Through deepening trials He endured to the end of His assignment: to atone for the sins of all humankind. His final words as He hung from the cross were, 'It is finished' (John 19:30). A commitment to endure to the end means that we . . . will persevere in pursuit of a worthy goal. It means that we will never give up on a loved one who has strayed. And it means that we will always cherish our eternal family relationships, even through difficult days of disease, disability, or death. ("The Mission and Ministry of Jesus Christ," from a devotional address given August 18, 1998, at Brigham Young University)

In that spirit, I add my prayer to that of Moroni for every leader who attempts to emulate the perfect example of our Lord Jesus Christ: "I am mindful of you always in my prayers, continually praying unto God the Father in the name of his Holy Child, Jesus, that he, through his infinite goodness and grace, will keep you through the endurance of faith on his name to the end" (Moroni 8:3).

Summary

Perhaps the most important competency of the Lord's divine leadership is shepherding. By following His enduring example as the good Shepherd, we can learn to love those we serve without reservation and avoid the timid behavior of the hireling or the aggressive nature of the sheepherder. The Savior is an exemplar, scholar, believer, seeker, disciple, teacher, and shepherd, and by following Him, we can improve our leadership ability to help those we serve return to our Father in Heaven.

SELECTED BIBLIOGRAPHY

Ballard, M. Russell, *Counseling with our Councils: Learning to Minister Together in the Church and in the Family* (Salt Lake City: Deseret Book, 1997).

Ballard, M. Russell, "O Be Wise," *Ensign*, November 2006.

Ballard, M. Russell, with Jeffrey R. Holland, David A. Bednar, Walter F. Gonzalez, and Julie B. Beck, "Panel Discussion," *Worldwide Leadership Training Meeting*, November 2010.

Bednar, David A., "The Atonement and the Journey of Mortality," *Ensign*, April 2012.

Benson, Ezra T., *God, Family, Country: Our Three Great Loyalties* (Salt Lake City: Deseret Book, 1974).

Benson, Ezra T., *The Teachings of Ezra Taft Benson* (Salt Lake City: Bookcraft, 1988).

Brewerton, Ted E., "Miracles," *New Era*, November 1990.

Clark, James R., *Messages of the First Presidency*, 6 volumes (Salt Lake City: Bookcraft, 1965–75).

Clark, Kim B., "Leadership," *Mormon Channel Radio*, Episode 29, October 2011.

Condie, Spencer J., "Reproving with Love," *Ensign*, August 1979.

Condie, Spencer J., "Some Scriptural Lessons on Leadership," *Ensign*, May 1990.

Cook, Gene R., *Raising Up a Family to the Lord* (Salt Lake City: Deseret Book, 1993).

Covey, Stephen R., "How Do You Get Others to Be Self-Motivated?" *Ensign*, February 1972.

Dew, Sheri L., *Ezra Taft Benson: A Biography* (Salt Lake City: Deseret Book, 1987).

Dyer, William G., "Personal Concern: A Principle of Leadership," *Ensign*, August 1972.

Dyer, William G., "Why, How, and How Not to Delegate: Some Hints for Home and Church," *Ensign*, August 1979.

Eyring, Henry B., "We Must Raise Our Sights," *Ensign*, September 2004.

Eyring, Henry B., "Our Perfect Example," *Ensign*, November 2009.

Fisher, Kimball, *Leading Self-Directed Work Teams* (New York: McGraw-Hill, Revised edition, 2000).

Funk, Ruth H., "Exceeding Young," *Ensign*, June 1977.

Handbook 2: Administering the Church (Salt Lake City: The Church of Jesus Christ of Latter-day Saints, 2010).

Holland, Jeffrey R., "The Lengthening Shadow of Peter," *Ensign*, September 1975.

Keyes, Randy, "Counseling Together in Marriage," *Ensign*, June 2012.

Kimball, Spencer W., "The Example of Abraham," *Ensign*, June 1975.

Kimball, Spencer W., "Jesus: The Perfect Leader," from an address delivered to the Young Presidents organization, Sun Valley, Idaho, January 15, 1977.

Lewis, C. S., *The Weight of Glory* (New York: Collier Books, Macmillan Publishing, 1980).

Monson, Thomas S., "Choose You This Day," *Ensign*, November 2004.

Nadauld, Margaret D., "The Joy of Womanhood," *Ensign*, November 2000.

Nadauld, Stephen D., *Principles of Priesthood Leadership* (Salt Lake City: Bookcraft, 1999).

Nelson, Russell M., "The Mission and Ministry of Jesus Christ," from a devotional address given August 18, 1998, at Brigham Young University.

Packer, Boyd K., *Teach Ye Diligently* (Salt Lake City: Deseret Book, 1975).

Packer, Boyd K., "Concluding Remarks," *Worldwide Leadership Training Meeting*, November 2010.

Perry, L. Tom, "Fatherhood, an Eternal Calling," *Ensign*, May 2004.

Perry, L. Tom and D. Todd Christofferson, "The Gospel Answers Life's Problems and Challenges," *Worldwide Leadership Training Meeting*, February 2012.

Perry, Lee Tom, *Righteous Influence: What Every Leader Should Know about Drawing on the Powers of Heaven* (Salt Lake City: Deseret Book, 2004).

Romney, Marion G., "Welfare Services: The Savior's Program," *Ensign*, October 1980.

Scott, Richard G., "Honor the Priesthood and Use It Well," *Ensign*, November 2008.

Smith, Joseph F., *Gospel Doctrine*, 11th edition (Salt Lake City: Deseret Book, 1959).

Tanner, N. Eldon, "Leading As the Savior Led," *Liahona*, January 1978.

Tucket, Glen, "Making Decisions and Feeding Sheep," *New Era,* January 1984.

Uchtdorf, Dieter F., "Faith of Our Father," *Ensign*, May 2008.

Widtsoe, John A., *Priesthood and Church Government in the Church of Jesus Christ of Latter-day Saints* (Salt Lake City: Deseret Book, 1939).

Widtsoe, John A., *Discourses of Brigham Young* (Salt Lake City: Deseret Book, 1954).

Wilkins, Alan L., *Developing Corporate Character* (San Francisco: Jossey-Bass, 1989).

Wilson, Larry Y., "Only upon the Principles of Righteousness," *Ensign*, May 2012.

Young, Brigham, "Varieties of Mind, Etc.," *Journal of Discourses*, Vol. 9 (London: Latter-day Saints' Book Depot, 1862), 121–25.

Young, Brigham, "The One-Man Power—Unity—Free Agency—Priesthood and Government, Etc.," *Journal of Discourses*, Vol. 14 (London: Latter-day Saints' Book Depot, 1862), 91–98.

——. *Teachings of Presidents of the Church: Ezra Taft Benson* (2014), "Chapter 19: Leadership," 241–51.

——. *Teaching the Gospel in the Savior's Way*, "Come, Follow Me: Learning Resources for Youth," http://www.lds.org.

——. "Tending the Flock: Teaching Leadership Skills to Youth," from an interview with President Dieter F. Uchtdorf and Elder M. Russell Ballard, *Liahona*, June 2008.

——. "The Gospel Answers Life's Problems and Challenges," *Worldwide Leadership Training Meeting*, 2012, with Elder L. Tom Perry and Elder D. Todd Christofferson.

NOTES

Notes

Notes

ABOUT THE AUTHOR

Kimball Fisher has spent over thirty years working as a consultant, specializing in training leaders to be more effective. He has worked with about 20 percent of the Fortune 100 corporations, as well as universities such as BYU, parts of the LDS Church, and government organizations, including the US Department of the Treasury and the staff office of the US Senate. He is the author and coauthor of the business bestsellers *Leading Self-Directed Work Teams* and *The Distance Manager* (with Mareen Fisher).

Brother Fisher received a leadership scholarship from BYU, where he graduated with a bachelor's degree in humanities and a master's degree in organizational behavior. He was the first recipient of the prestigious William G. Dyer Award for outstanding contributions to the field of management and has served as a missionary in the Japan Sapporo Mission, elders quorum president, bishop's counselor, Scoutmaster, high priests group leader, high councilor, bishop, and stake president's counselor. He and his wife live in Portland, Oregon.

You can reach him at www.kimballfisher.com.

SCAN to visit

WWW.KIMBALLFISHER.COM